All Sides of the I

Activities for Cooperative Jigsaw Groups

Elizabeth Coelho
North York Board of Education
Toronto

Lise Winer
McGill University
Montréal

Judy Winn-Bell Olsen
City College of San Francisco

Alta Book Center Publishers
San Francisco, California USA

Project Editor: Helen Munch

Copy Editor: Marc Lecard

Production/Design: E. Carol Gee

Illustrations: C. Buck Reynolds

Cover Design: Kathleen Peterson

The original ideas for "Industrial Accident" (pp. 79-100) and "Saving the Biramichi River" (pp. 101-126) were contributed by Neville Coelho.

ISBN 1-882483-72-3

Alta Book Center Publishers - San Francisco USA

Contents

Continued

Contents *Continued*

All Sides of the Issue

Activities for Cooperative Jigsaw Groups

Teacher's Guide

Introduction

About This Book

All Sides of the Issue: Activities for Cooperative Jigsaw Groups is a teacher resource book of small group activities based on the principles of cooperative learning and the Jigsaw approach. The activities focus on issues of social importance, designed to help students develop both language and social studies skills. *All Sides of the Issue* consists of a Teacher's Guide and duplicatable student materials for the seven activities presented in the book.

Audience

All Sides of the Issue is for language development and social studies teachers with adolescent and adult students whose native language may or may not be English. Many of these students need help with their reading and discussion skills in a wide variety of academic and nonacademic tasks. As can be seen from the Contents (pp. iii–iv), the readings and activities are suitable for use in areas besides language arts and social studies.

All Sides of the Issue is written for multilevel high school, adult school or community college classes in which students are reading several grades below their expected grade level. Student reading levels may range from about third to seventh grade for one or more of the following reasons:

- students are unaware of specific reading skills and strategies that can be applied to specific reading tasks;
- students have a limited vocabulary in English, especially if English is not their native language;
- students are not members of the majority cultural group and do not identify with much of what is read in class;
- students are new to the American education system, or are re-entry students, and are uncomfortable with a teaching/learning style that emphasizes student-directed tasks, group work, and open-ended questions;
- students lack confidence in their ability to work without strong teacher supervision; they need structured confidence-building activities.

Organization and Content

All Sides of the Issue is divided into two parts: the Teacher's Guide and the duplicatable student materials. The Introduction to the Teacher's Guide, which you are now reading, presents general information about the book. Chapter 1, "Cooperative Learning and the Jigsaw Approach," explores the pedagogical foundation of these two educational practices. Chapter 2, "Getting Started," suggests ways to introduce cooperative learning strategies into classroom routines and activities. Chapter 3, "The Jigsaw Classroom," focuses on the Jigsaw method of classroom instruction and curriculum organization. And chapter 4, "Notes to the Teacher," provides specific notes for the seven cooperative activities that form the remaining portion of the book.

The second part of *All Sides of the Issue* contains all of the duplicatable student exercise material and evaluation sheets for the two introductory activities (a Jigsaw Drawing and a Jigsaw Word Puzzle), and for the five Jigsaw activities ("The Letter of the Law," "Heart Victim Can't Stay," "Industrial Accident," "Saving the Biramichi River," and "Who Discovered America?"). An answer key is also provided for certain of the reading skills exercises.

The innovative materials in *All Sides of the Issue* provide students with stimulating, content-based reading, discussion tasks, and problem-solving activities on a wide range of topics across the curriculum. The activities promote effective communication and interaction in multilevel groups, and assist the teacher in meeting students' individual needs. The duplicatable student materials offer students opportunities to develop the following reading strategies and academic skills:

Reading Strategies

- reading for the main idea (skimming)
- reading for specific information (scanning)
- checking the text for details
- making inferences and predictions beyond the text
- inferring word meaning from context
- evaluating information and forming an opinion
- asking appropriate questions to clarify a text

Academic Skills

- preparing and delivering an oral paraphrase of a text
- asking/answering questions and discussing information
- cooperating and interacting with a group on shared learning tasks
- synthesizing data for a written response
- acquiring background information on common American concepts, themes, values, and institutions

As students develop both their reading strategies and oral skills, they will be able to interact successfully with native speakers outside the ESL classroom and assume greater control over their own language learning.

How to Use This Book

If you are completely new to cooperative learning in general and to the Jigsaw approach in particular, read on. Chapter 1, "Cooperative Learning and the Jigsaw Approach," contains specific information for you. If you are familiar with cooperative learning but have not yet begun working with students in cooperative groups, begin with chapter 2, "Getting Started." If you are already familiar with cooperative learning and have worked with students in cooperative groups but not with the Jigsaw approach, go to chapter 3, "The Jigsaw Classroom." And if you are familiar with all of the ideas and information presented in chapters 1–3, go directly to chapter 4, "Notes to the Teacher," for the activities in this book.

Chapter 1

Cooperative Learning and the Jigsaw Approach

All Sides of the Issue is based on the cooperative learning approach to classroom and curriculum organization. The specific strategy used is known as the Jigsaw method.

Cooperative Learning: An Overview

Definition

Cooperative learning is an approach to education and a repertoire of teaching strategies based on the philosophy that students can learn effectively in small groups. The groups and the learning experiences are organized so that 1) students become accountable for each other's learning, and 2) students acquire effective group skills and learning strategies. In cooperatively organized classrooms, it is to everyone's benefit to have everyone succeed. To that end, students learn how to assist each other.

Cooperative learning is qualitatively different from what is often called "group work." In group work, students sit and sometimes work together. Student contributions may be unequal, and some students may not contribute, participate, or learn at all. This kind of group work, which does not create interdependence and accountability, often produces results similar to those of the traditional classroom. That is to say, the gap between high and low achievers remains more or less constant or grows wider in each successive grade, while the different racial and cultural groups in the school grow farther and farther apart. By the time students reach the senior grades, there is very little positive interaction among the groups.

In contrast, cooperative learning restructures the traditional classroom into small, carefully planned learning groups to provide opportunities for all students to work together and to learn from each other.

Rationale and Benefits

There are several reasons why cooperative learning is both needed and successful.

Rationale

Across the United States parents and educators are becoming more and more concerned about the quality of education received in the nation's schools. Evidence shows that many students leave school unable to read and write at a level that allows them to function effectively in an increasingly information-oriented, technologically driven society. Particular racial or ethnic groups appear to be experiencing more difficulty than others. Cooperative learning can and does help these groups and others in the school environment.

The United States is a multiracial, multicultural society in which people have to tolerate, respect, and work with others from different backgrounds. Employers are in greater need now than ever of flexible, cooperative individuals who can work with others and learn new tasks. With family members spending less time together now than they did generations ago, the school is the principal socializing agent in many students' lives. Cooperative learning provides students opportunities to develop effective social skills that will enable them to become well-adjusted members of society.

Benefits

Many studies have demonstrated that increased learning takes place in a classroom that is organized cooperatively. The academic gains are greatest for minority students and lower achievers. Such students, it is theorized, are more cooperatively oriented than their mainstream peers (Kagan 1986). However, high achievers do at least as well as (and often better than) their peers in traditionally structured classrooms.

Studies have also consistently shown an improvement in race relations among students after they have experienced cooperative learning. According to Robert Slavin," . . . the effects of student teams on interracial friendship and related variables may be the most important of the outcomes. . . . Fostering interracial cooperation is by far the most effective means of improving racial attitudes and behaviors in schools" (Slavin 1980).

Cooperative learning has been shown to enhance students' self-esteem, a factor closely correlated to academic achievement. Studies have revealed that team learning "greatly increased helping behavior, perceptions of giving and receiving help, and a sense of being able to cope with classroom studies" (Sharan 1980). It seems probable then that students learn to value cooperative, noncompetitive behavior not only in academic group tasks, but in their relationships in general.

Cooperative learning methods give teachers, especially those at the middle and secondary levels, the necessary tools and strategies to provide the structured, organized opportunities that encourage exploratory talk among nonjudgmental peers. Research in language and learning suggests that such exploratory talk helps students to internalize new ideas and formulate new concepts in every subject area. It also fosters the development of higher-level thinking skills such as analysis, evaluation, and synthesis of information and ideas.

The Jigsaw Approach

Definition

Several tried and tested strategies for effective learning in small groups are being widely practiced as part of a movement toward cooperative or collaborative learning in North America, Israel, Britain, Australia, and other parts of the world. The activities presented in *All Sides of the Issue* represent one such strategy, known as the Jigsaw. "Jigsaw" refers to a particular method of cooperative classroom organization and instruction devised and documented by Elliot Aronson (Aronson et al. 1978) and others to enhance academic performance and improve interracial relations in the classroom.

In the Jigsaw classroom, students in small groups depend on one another for information needed to learn a topic, complete a task, or solve a problem. Each student in the group becomes an expert on a particular topic or section of a topic, and thus has a different piece of the puzzle (hence the term "Jigsaw"). Although each student's information is independently comprehensible, the ultimate learning goal is for everyone in the group to have the whole set of information. It is therefore each group member's task to share his or her piece of information so that all the students know all of the material. In Jigsaw then, students are individually accountable for learning their own material and for sharing their information effectively with other group members.

Rationale and Benefits

Although the Jigsaw method of classroom organization was not designed specifically for second-language instruction, it is admirably suited to the ESL classroom because it fosters purposeful, task-oriented communication. The information-sharing and discussion process helps students to acquire and refine their oral strategies for a wide variety of language functions. The increased opportunities for interaction allow students more practice in language functions such as narrating, explaining, comparing, asking for information or clarification, and expressing opinions.

In mainstream classes, consisting of heterogeneous groups of native and non-native speakers of English, ESL students interact with peers who serve as language models. Opportunities to question and to negotiate meaning increase. The native speakers modify their language to make themselves understood, and the English-language learners model their own language use on that of their peers to make themselves understood in turn. All students (native speakers and second-language learners) are learning and extending their language while using it. Students become successful communicators because they have a genuine need to communicate effectively.

All Sides of the Issue

The structure of the Jigsaw units in this book demands that each student read and rehearse material with a specific purpose in mind: to be able to teach or tell the other group members about the main points and important details of a particular piece of information. Retelling or paraphrasing the main points of what has been read is a very effective teaching/learning strategy for improving students' reading comprehension. In the conventional classroom, the teacher is the audience and must share time with each student. In the Jigsaw classroom, one student's group of three other students is the audience, and there is ample time for sharing and discussion.

Chapter 2

Getting Started

As indicated in chapter 1, a key element of cooperative learning is the building and fostering of effective groups. Cooperative learning groups and the techniques they employ can be incorporated into the regular classroom routine in many ways and for several reasons: to increase student comfort, to provide a warm and positive atmosphere, and to provide more opportunities for students to develop their language skills.

For those unfamiliar with small cooperative group work, this chapter offers suggestions on forming groups, building a team, introducing accountability, and developing cooperative group skills. As the basic procedures become familiar, portions of an existing curriculum may be adapted to cooperative learning strategies to increase student involvement.

Forming Groups

The formation of cooperative groups will vary according to the activity, the number of students in the class, and the students' abilities. Most cooperative groups work best with three to four students. Having more than four students in a group makes it difficult for everyone to participate fully. The activities in *All Sides of the Issue* involve four students per group (see chapter 4, pp. 15–32).

Most students, left on their own, will naturally form groups with others from the same cultural, linguistic, and/or socioeconomic background, and with those having the same interests, proficiency level, or the same sex. Research indicates, however, that all students benefit more when cooperative learning groups are as heterogeneous as possible.

The formation of heterogeneous groups may be influenced by such factors as regular versus open enrollment, or predictable versus fluctuating attendance. If classroom attendance is relatively stable, groups can be carefully planned and students assigned to groups in advance. Once assigned, students should work in the same group for a period of several weeks to allow for the development of a group identity and team spirit. Students should not remain in the same groups the entire year or semester, however. Participation in a variety of groups can help accustom students to the types of transitions they will encounter later on (to new schools, to the world of work).

If attendance varies from day to day or from week to week, groups can be formed on a random basis for each cooperative activity. The easiest way to form random groups is to have students "count off" as you, the teacher, point to each one. For example, in a class of 25, for groups of four, have students stand and count off by six—"one, two, three, four, five, six, one, two, three, four, five, six, one . . ." Be sure that each student repeats his or her number as a means of remembering it. When students have finished counting off, have all the number ones identify themselves by raising their hands; then have the number twos, threes, fours, fives, and sixes do likewise. After checking all the numbers, assign each numbered group to a special place in the classroom. ("Okay, ones—sit over there; twos—stand back there; threes . . .") Any latecomers or students with leftover numbers can be added to one of the original six groups.

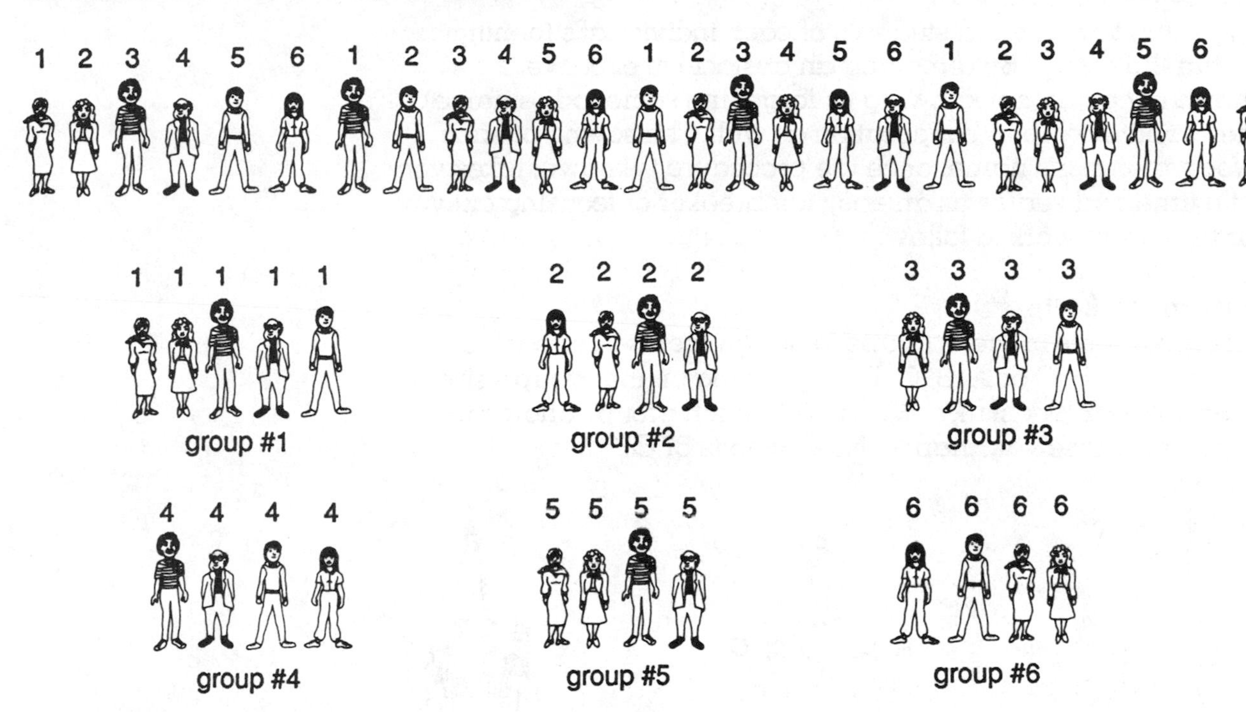

Once students are in groups, inequities can be spotted and adjustments made. For example, are all the newcomers in one or two groups? Did most of the more proficient students end up together? In any group, are there more than two students who speak the same language? Some switching of students may be necessary to avoid homogeneous groups. Heterogeneous group formation becomes easier as students get used to the count-off procedure and to individual student similarities, differences, strengths, and weaknesses.

Building a Team

The essence of successful cooperative group work is the building of a group identity and team spirit. Whether the group is newly formed (strangers meeting together for the first time) or ongoing, the need exists for a warm-up activity to establish or to reestablish that necessary human connection among the group members. A number of warm-up and team-building activities can be used. The ones that follow are relatively short and especially appropriate for students who do not know each other well and/or who are new to cooperative group work.

Learning or Reviewing Names

- Bring index cards and marking pens to class and have students make their own name tags. Names should be printed in letters large enough for all group members to read.

- Leave the name tags in a designated area of the classroom and instruct students to wear their name tags whenever they are in class. At the end of class all name tags should be returned.
- When students work in their cooperative groups, have them take turns reading and saying aloud the name of each student in the group. Students should not say their own name aloud unless someone is having a problem pronouncing it.

Name tags remind students of each individual's identity within the group. By removing an obstacle to effective communication (not knowing or forgetting somebody's name), they facilitate group cooperation as well. The saying of each group member's name, once the procedure is known, takes very little time and serves as an easy ice-breaker or focusing activity for the group work to follow.

Assigning Letters

- Ask students in their groups to assign themselves each a letter—A, B, C or A, B, C, D, depending on the group's size.
- Spot check by asking "Who is A in each group? Show me, please. Raise your hands. Now, who is B? C?"

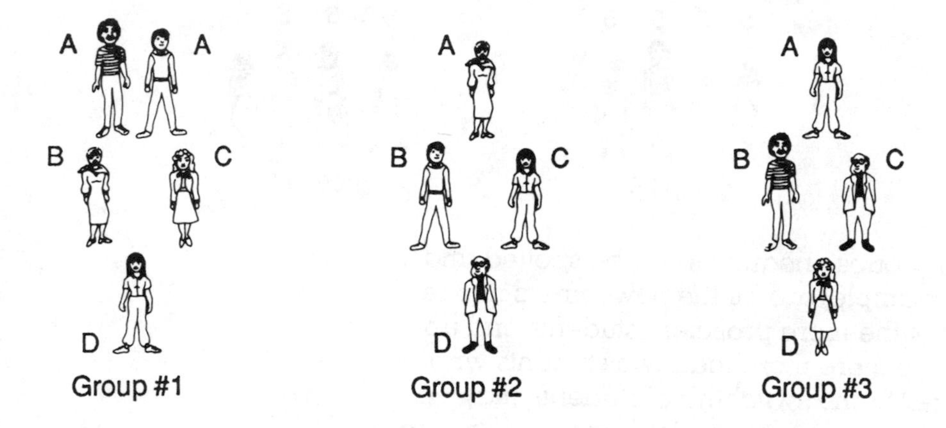

The number-letter combination (from the initial count-off and in-group letter assignment, p. 7) facilitates group identification and later serves as an important tool in the effective management of cooperative and Jigsaw groups (see chapter 3, pp. 12–14).

Getting to Know You

Have students establish a relationship with one another by sharing simple information in a structured or an unstructured way.

Directed interviews

- Assign an easy interview task that allows students to use familiar grammatical structures and to elicit information that is fairly straightforward and not too personal: "In the next four minutes, I want you to get different information from each member of the group. Find out A's first language, B's birthday, C's family name, and D's favorite sport."

- Follow the interviews with a spot check to see that students did as asked: "Who is C in this group? Please tell me what A's first language is. Okay. Now, in this group, who is B? What is D's favorite sport?"

Open-ended interviews

- Ask students in their groups to find out what things they have in common. Students may discover that although they differ racially, linguistically, culturally, and in ways some may prefer not to acknowledge, they have more in common than they thought.
- As with the directed interviews, follow up with a spot check ("Okay, let me hear from the A's this time: What did your group members have in common?") to keep students on task and to affirm the activity's credibility. The spot check also enables groups to hear what other groups are doing while allowing for assessment of individual students' oral control of grammar, vocabulary, and pronunciation.

Open-ended interviews, if repeated, help build trust among group members and may result in the students beginning to share more personal information. Public sharing of such information is not necessary, however.

Introducing Accountability

Some of the preceding team-building activities have recommended spot checks to see that students have done as requested (see pp. 7–8). Such checks, made a regular part of the activity, help students develop an awareness of their individual responsibilities and accountabilities in a group situation and help foster cooperation. More proficient students are motivated to help the less proficient, while all students are encouraged to pay full attention and to participate in the group activity.

The following classroom activities for language development can easily be converted into group activities in which each student is held accountable.

Vocabulary

- Following the introduction of new vocabulary, divide the list of words or phrases so that each group member receives a portion of it.
- Explain to students that they are each responsible for learning the meaning, pronunciation, and usage of the vocabulary on their list. (Students can work independently at their desks or meet in groups at specially designated letter "stations" in the classroom, such as the A station, B station, and so on.)
- When all students have finished mastering their vocabulary lists, have them teach the individual words or phrases to the other members of their group with the help of flashcards, cloze exercises, charades, or any other techniques that appear to work.

Dictation

- Select a passage for dictation that students have already read and comprehended.
- Divide the words or sentences in the passage so that each group member receives a portion.
- Tell students that they must each learn the correct pronunciation of their words or sentences. (As with the vocabulary activity on p. 9, students can work together in groups at previously designated letter stations where the correct pronunciation can first be modelled, then practiced.)
- When students have finished practicing the pronunciation of their words or sentences, have them return to their groups and dictate their sentences (in order) to each other.

Grammar

- Using a multiple-choice, fill-in-the-blank, or transformational exercise, assign each group a portion of the exercise.
- Explain to the groups that they are to do their portion of the exercise together, checking the answers and making any adjustments. As the groups finish their portion, they may continue with the rest of the exercise.
- When all groups have finished their portion, have a representative from each group write that group's answers on the chalkboard or dictate the answers aloud.
- When all answers have been given, distribute copies of the answers to the exercise, one copy per group. Group members can check their answers against the list read aloud, or individually read their answers aloud to be checked against the board list.

Discussion

- Have students sit in groups for a typical teacher-dominated class (a lecture or class discussion).
- When a question is asked (by the teacher or a student), have the groups consider and then discuss the question to see if an answer will emerge. Encourage the more proficient to help the less proficient students.
- After the groups have finished their discussion, ask each group's representative (A, B, C) to share the group's answer.

Accountability can be built into regular classroom management tasks as well as other curriculum-related activities. For example, A's can be asked to collect the homework for the day, B's can find out who was absent and distribute the previous day's assignment, and so on.

Accountability can also be incorporated into students' evaluations of their individual group experiences. Such evaluations encourage self-reflection and discussion while helping to build the students' social and linguistic skills. (See p. 11, "Developing Cooperative Skills.")

A sample personal evaluation form for students working in cooperative groups is found on p. 126 of the duplicatable student materials. This form may be used with any of the introductory and Jigsaw activities in this book and with other cooperative learning group activities.

Developing Cooperative Skills

Students accustomed to working independently in competitive educational systems may initially find it difficult to work cooperatively as part of a group. Apart from lacking experience in working with others on learning tasks, they may not know how to express themselves in English in ways that facilitate the group process. Cooperative group skills include the following language functions and social skills:

- encouraging, praising, and showing appreciation
- actively participating through taking turns, contributing ideas, checking for understanding, or seeking clarification
- managing conflict by expressing disagreement, offering suggestions, and diffusing tension

Cooperative group skills can be analyzed in terms of the specific language functions they require. This language can then be modelled, discussed, and practiced in a variety of contexts, taking into account the relationship of the speakers, the appropriateness of their registers, and any nonverbal signals. For example, students can list useful phrases and nonverbal expressions for taking turns during a discussion, then practice using them in their cooperative groups and/or during the next class discussion.

Cooperative skills exercise sheets that identify one skill and focus on its corresponding language are among the duplicatable student materials found in the second part of *All Sides of the Issue*.

Chapter 3

The Jigsaw Classroom

Chapter 1 presented an overview of cooperative learning and the Jigsaw approach. Chapter 2 provided suggestions and activities for introducing cooperative learning strategies into the classroom. Chapter 3 describes in greater detail the Jigsaw classroom and how students function in Jigsaw groups.

The Teacher and the Jigsaw Classroom

The Jigsaw classroom is highly structured, with carefully selected student groups. The groups are formed as described in chapter 2 (pp. 6–7) and should be as heterogeneous as possible. In the Jigsaw classroom, the role of the teacher changes significantly from agent of control and disseminator of all knowledge to catalyst and adviser. Once the teacher has assigned groups and topics, the students assume control of the activity. Responsibility for participation becomes the students' once materials are distributed and the activity is underway. The teacher is then free to offer assistance and individual attention to those students in need of it.

The Students and Jigsaw Groups

Once students have been assigned to groups, they are each assigned a letter (A, B, C or A, B, C, D) according to their language proficiency and to the arrangement of the student materials for a particular Jigsaw activity. In the five Jigsaw activities in *All Sides of the Issue*, the letters correspond to the reading levels of the four texts for each activity (two low intermediate and two intermediate) and to the order of presentation of the texts (A, B, C, D). The letter/reading-level correspondences change from one activity to the next. For example, in the first Jigsaw activity "The Letter of the Law," the four reading texts are identified in the "Notes to the Teacher" (p. 20) as follows: A=intermediate, B=low intermediate, C=intermediate, and D=low intermediate. Students are assigned A, B, C, or D according to their reading level and are given the corresponding reading text.

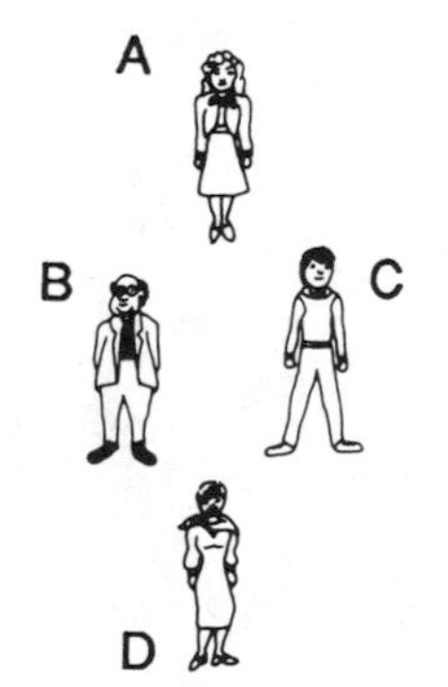

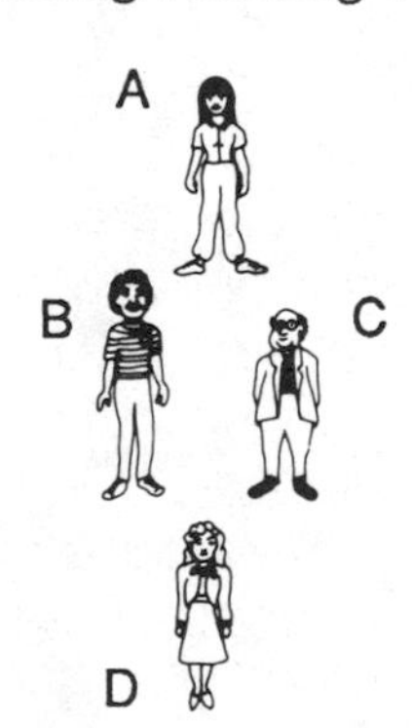

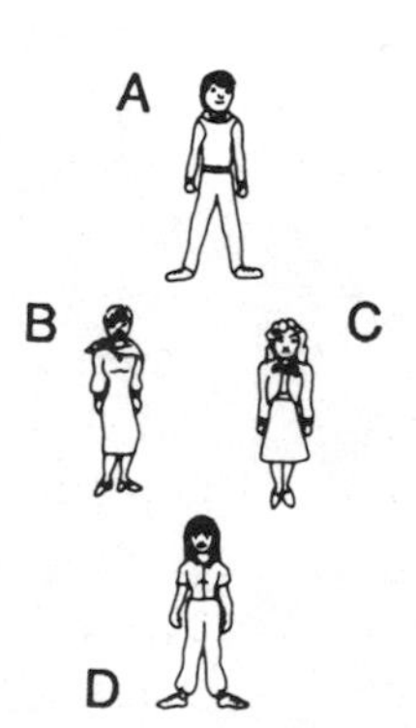

Students assigned the same letter and text—A, for example—become "experts" on the A material for their group. The experts form their own groups to master the same material. So, in a class of 12 working on "The Letter of the Law" three B students and three D students would form two separate low intermediate expert groups on the B and D reading texts. Three A and three C students would form two separate intermediate expert groups on the A and C reading texts.

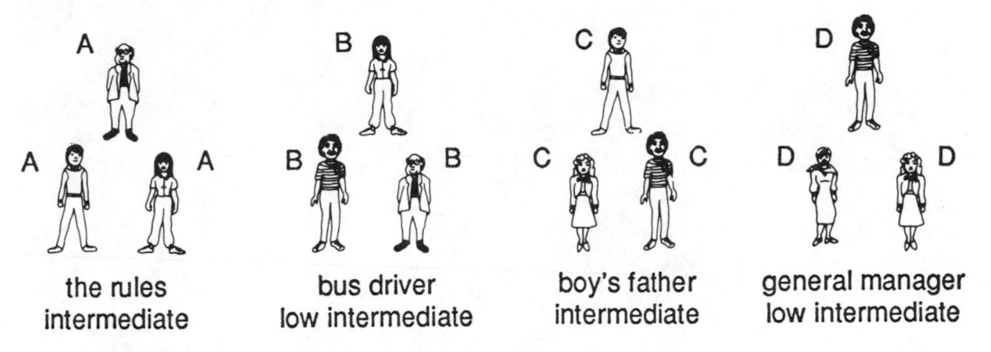

How Students Work in the Expert Groups

In the letter-coded expert groups, students work together on the same reading text, completing the reading skills exercises, and rehearsing and presenting to one another the material for their individual Jigsaw group presentations. The teacher, as facilitator, circulates from expert group to expert group, discussing and checking responses to the exercises, and helping students help each other with their presentations. Guiding one another, students learn how to recognize what information is irrelevant or has been omitted, how to comment on pace, audibility of delivery, pronunciation, body language, and how to use specific presentation techniques, such as writing key words on the chalkboard and so on.

How Students Work in Jigsaw Groups

When all students working in the expert groups feel they know their material and are ready to share it, they return to their respective Jigsaw groups. Each student—A, B, C, and D—then tells the other Jigsaw group members about the content of his or her reading text, consulting the text for details only. The students compare and check their information with one another and exchange any opinions in an attempt to reach some conclusions about the reading text. The teacher guides discussion toward a consensus or a majority/minority view, or toward the solution of a problem. At the end of the discussion, each group reports its results (and the group's reasoning) to the class. Since most of the activities in *All Sides of the Issue* are open-ended with no one "correct" solution, groups will most likely reach several different conclusions. However, correct responses are expected for some of the duplicatable reading skills exercises such as True, False, or ?, Find the Words, Find the Meaning, and Think About It that follow each of the lettered reading texts. For this reason, an answer key has been provided (pp. 151–154).

Following the in-group discussions and class reports, each group should review the activity and exercise material prior to taking a quiz on it. The quiz is the same for all students and is based on the content of all four reading texts (A, B, C, D) and on the Jigsaw group discussions. (See chapter 4, pp. 15–32 for additional information about Jigsaw quizzes in this book.)

Chapter 4

Notes to the Teacher

The preceding three chapters have dealt with the principles of cooperative and Jigsaw learning (chapter 1), practical suggestions for introducing students to cooperative learning groups (chapter 2), and a description of the Jigsaw classroom (chapter 3). Chapter 4 contains general information regarding the seven activities in *All Sides of the Issue* and specific notes for each of the activities.

Duplicatable Student Materials

Each of the two introductory activities and the five Jigsaw activities contains student materials for duplication. The "Notes to the Teacher" for each activity specify the pages that need to be duplicated in advance. In addition to maps, drawings, puzzles, and the reading text, the duplicatable materials include reading skills exercises, quizzes, cooperative skills sheets, and group evaluation sheets. The exercises and quizzes are keyed to specific Jigsaw activities, but the cooperative skills exercises and the evaluation sheets following specific activities may be used interchangeably with any or all of the introductory or Jigsaw activities in the book. For example, the cooperative skills sheet, "Seeking Clarification" that follows the student materials for the introductory Jigsaw Word Puzzle may be used with either or both of the introductory activities.

The Introductory Activities

The purpose of the two introductory activities is to acquaint students with the principles of cooperative learning through performance of specific tasks: a Jigsaw drawing and a Jigsaw word puzzle. Unlike the graded Jigsaw activities that follow (with the exception of "The Letter of the Law," which is ungraded), the introductory activities are ungraded. The letter designations for the drawing and word puzzle refer only to the order of presentation of the duplicatable student materials. There is no letter/reading-level correspondence for the introductory activity materials.

The introductory activities may be introduced in conjunction with other activities suggested in chapter 2, "Getting Started," or they may be presented prior to beginning the Jigsaw activities in this book. Check the Resources list on pp. 33–34 for additional books that describe activities (such as cooperative games) to supplement the introductory activities in *All Sides of the Issue*.

The Jigsaw Activities

The five Jigsaw activities that follow the introductory activities are reading-based, emphasizing issues of social importance. While the format of each activity is similar, there are some differences in the length, complexity, and focus of each one. The first Jigsaw activity, "The Letter of the Law," for example, is shorter than the subsequent four Jigsaw activities. It serves as an introductory Jigsaw activity. The remaining Jigsaw activities progress in difficulty. Again, depending on the teacher's and students' familiarity with the Jigsaw approach and on interest in a particular subject or skills topic, the Jigsaw activities following "The Letter of the Law" may be presented sequentially or in another order. Consult the "Notes to the Teacher" for each activity to determine the best presentation order for you and your class.

The Jigsaw Readings

The readings for the five Jigsaw activities (pp. 35–150) are controlled for vocabulary and sentence length. Unfamiliar words are introduced with strong contextual support and, in some cases, visual aids are provided. Pre-reading questions and activities also serve as aids to comprehension.

As with the introductory activities, the Jigsaw readings have been assigned letters—A, B, C, D,—that reflect their order of presentation within each Jigsaw group. In addition, the readings are graded at two levels: low intermediate and intermediate. "Low intermediate" corresponds to a reading level of grades 3 and 4 on standardized tests, or level 2 in most ESL readers (Longman, Prentice-Hall/Regents, Oxford). "Intermediate" corresponds to reading levels of grades 4 through 6 on standardized tests, or level 3 in ESL readers.

Each Jigsaw activity features two readings at the low intermediate level and two at the intermediate level. The individual "Notes to the Teacher" for each specific activity indicate the reading level of each reading text (A, B, C, D). The letter/reading-level designations change from one activity to the next.

The Reading Skills Exercises

Each Jigsaw activity also features several duplicatable exercises designed to help students understand the readings and to work with the vocabulary and issues involved. The four most frequent reading skills exercises are described as follows:

True, False, or ?

The statements in this exercise are both factual and inferential. Some cover the main point of the reading, some focus on details. The **?** option is for students to choose when they feel they lack sufficient information.

Find the Words

This exercise provides general definitions and refers students to the reading for specific matching words.

Find the Meaning

This exercise presents specific vocabulary from the reading and refers students to the reading to infer general definitions. Students should be encouraged to use contextual clues to *guess* the meanings of words. Dictionary use should be discouraged.

Think About It

These open-ended questions require students to evaluate some of the information they have read. Expert groups should discuss these questions before writing their individual answers. When checking student responses, comment only on students' accuracy of comprehension and reading. Leave grammar and spelling for another lesson.

In addition to the above exercises, two Jigsaw activities each feature another exercise: Find the Details (in "How to Save the Biramichi River") and Study the Map (in "Who Discovered America?").

Answers to the reading skills exercises appear in the Answer Key, pp. 151–154.

Introductory Activity 1: Jigsaw Drawing

This small-group activity expands the concept and practice of cooperation by asking students to draw the missing parts of a picture. Students practice drawing lines and shapes, giving and responding to directions, and clarifying instructions.

Warm-Up (the same day or a day ahead)

- Make a transparency of the Base Picture on p. 37 for use with an overhead projector, or duplicate copies of the Base Picture, one per group.
- Divide the class into heterogeneous groups of four. (See chapter 2, pp. 6–7, on forming groups.)
- Display the transparency or distribute the copies of the Base Picture.
- Review questions 1–6 at the top of the Base Picture page and have students discuss them, first in their groups and then with the whole class. For question 6, suggest situations in which clarification or encouragement might be needed, or ask students for suggestions. Offer some examples of clarifying phrases ("Would you say that again, slowly, please?" "Did you say _____ or _____ ?") and words of encouragement ("That's the idea." "You've got it now.") Additional clarifying language is included on the Jigsaw Drawing Vocabulary sheet (p. 38).
- Elicit, review, and practice vocabulary appropriate for a description of the Base Picture. Write the words and phrases on the board as students produce them. Additional vocabulary, some of which may duplicate your board list, appears on the Jigsaw Drawing Vocabulary sheet (p. 38).

Preparation

- Duplicate copies of the Jigsaw Drawing Vocabulary sheet (p. 38), one per group, sets of drawings A, B, C, and D (pp. 39–42), and the Master Picture (p. 43), one per group (optional). You might also want to duplicate group copies of the cooperative skills sheet, "Seeking Clarification" (p. 49) for use as a follow-up to the drawing activity.
- Continue with the same Warm-Up groups or, if you did the Warm-Up on the preceding day, divide the class into the same

heterogeneous groups of four. Integrate any newcomers in the class as necessary.

Procedure

- Distribute the copies of the Jigsaw Drawing Vocabulary sheet, one per group. Review and practice using the words, phrases, and questions presented, and answer any student questions.
- Reminding students of their work with the Base Picture, display one set of Jigsaw drawings and explain that each student in a group will receive a different incomplete drawing—A, B, C, or D. Together the four drawings form a complete picture, the Master Picture, which you have. Each separate drawing shares some details with the other drawings. These common details are drawn in dotted lines. Each drawing also has some special details of its own. These special details are drawn in solid lines.
- Without looking at each other's drawings, the students in each group must complete their drawings by listening to each other's descriptions of what to draw. Students will take turns describing their drawings so that the other group members can draw in the four missing details on their own papers.
- Following your explanation, distribute the sets of drawings, one per group. Review the activity directions and answer any questions.

Follow-Up

- When students in a particular group have completed their drawings, instruct them to line up their four drawings for comparison. Students may alter their individual drawings at this time based on group discussion and comparison.
- When *all* students have completed their drawings, you may want to have an art show and put up all the pictures for students to compare. You can also display the Base Picture again, using the overhead projector, and have students instruct you in drawing in the missing details.
- As a wrap-up, display the Master Picture using the overhead projector, or distribute copies of the Master Picture, one per group.
- Review questions 1–5 at the top of the Master Picture page and have students discuss them, first in their groups and then with the whole class. Answers to questions 1–4 should be fairly obvious from the information in the picture. Encourage students to examine the picture carefully to provide the details necessary for the answers. Answers to question 5 will vary.
- To finish the activity, ask students to describe their experiences and feelings when working cooperatively in a group, especially if this is students' first time working in cooperative groups. Encourage students to talk about the difficulties as well as the benefits of working cooperatively. See if students can identify any particular problems and possible solutions.
- If you duplicated copies of the cooperative skills sheet, "Seeking Clarification" you may want to distribute them for group work at this time.

Extension Work

Create your own content-related Jigsaw drawings from other pictorial sources (science and history textbooks, for example) as a means of incorporating and extending cooperative Jigsaw strategies into the curriculum.

Introductory Activity 2: Jigsaw Word Puzzle

This Jigsaw readiness activity is designed to demonstrate and promote the effectiveness of cooperative group learning. Students focus on cooperative behavior and on the skills required for the successful exchange, clarification, and confirmation of information.

Warm-Up (a day ahead)

Do Introductory Activity 1 and/or introduce students to some relatively easy word puzzles from the local newspaper, magazines, game books or school textbooks.

Preparation

- Duplicate sets of the word puzzle (A, B, C, D) on pp. 44–47 group copies of the Answer Key (p. 48) and the cooperative skills sheet, "Seeking Clarification," (p. 49).
- Divide the class into heterogeneous Jigsaw groups of four. (See chapter 2, pp. 6–7, on forming groups.)

Procedure

- Explain to students that the purpose of the activity is to help them work better in small groups and to read and discuss material more easily.
- Hold up one word puzzle (A, B, C, or D) and explain that each student in a group will receive one puzzle, each with a different set of clues. Together the sets of clues reveal a hidden word in the completed puzzle, a copy of which you have (the Answer Key). Without showing each other their puzzles, students will take turns telling each other their clues to words 1, 2, and so on, until each group member has completed the puzzle.
- Following your explanation, distribute the word puzzles. Review the activity directions and answer any questions.

Follow-Up

- When all groups have completed their puzzles, distribute the Answer Key and have students compare their results.
- Discuss with students the concept of a "jigsaw puzzle" and how it cannot be completed until all of the missing information is known.
- Discuss the various linguistic signals students used to get information from each other or to clarify or confirm what they heard: "Huh?"; "What?"; "Whadja say?"; "Did you say . . . ?"; "Would you spell that?" Mention any nonverbal signals that you observed.

- Distribute the cooperative skills sheet, "Seeking Clarification," and have students discuss and reach consensus on the language for the indicated functions. Ask students to decide if some strategies are more cooperative, more polite, and less "blaming" than others. Ask each group to make a list of verbal and nonverbal strategies they consider acceptable in their group. Have students indicate which strategies they would or would not use in the classroom when asking the teacher to repeat, clarify, or confirm something. Post the list for future class reference.

Extension Work

Introduce other cooperative games and activities to further develop students' cooperative attitudes and skills. Consult the Resources list (pp. 33–34) for publications containing suggestions for team-building activities and cooperative board games.

Jigsaw Activity 1: The Letter of the Law

This introductory Jigsaw activity is shorter than the four Jigsaw activities that follow it. Missing are the reading skills exercises and vocabulary development present in the other Jigsaw activities. Upon completion of this activity, students should be ready for the remaining full-length Jigsaw activities.

The presentation and sequence remain the same for all five Jigsaw activities; however, the pre-reading questions, directed discussion, and follow-up activities differ and are specific to each Jigsaw activity.

Synopsis

A young boy has to walk home after a bus driver refuses to give him a transfer.

Roles and Reading Levels

A	intermediate	a description of the rules of the Metropolitan Transportation Company
B	low intermediate	the bus driver's story
C	intermediate	the boy's father's story
D	low intermediate	the general manager's story

Preparation

- Duplicate sets of "The Letter of the Law" readings (A, B, C, D, pp. 50–57), and copies of the quiz (p. 58) for each Jigsaw group and the cooperative skills sheet "Working in Groups" (p. 59) for each student.
- Have students meet together in their expert groups. (See chapter 3, pp. 12–13, on forming expert groups.)
- Distribute the readings—A, B, C, or D—to each expert group.

Procedure

Pre-reading

- Allow students no more than 30 seconds to find the answer to this question: "What is your story about?" (Answers: a problem on a bus, the transportation system in Springfield, how to use a transfer.)
- Compare answers and discuss the difference between *skimming* for the main idea and reading the entire text in detail. Emphasize that effective readers read no more than necessary for a specific purpose.

Reading with a purpose

- Explain to students that there are four different readings, each one containing different information about the topic.
- Ask students to skim their readings again to determine whose story (or what piece of information) they have. Write the students' responses on the chalkboard: the rules of the SMTC, the bus driver's story, the boy's father's story, or the general manager's story.

Reading for details

- Instruct students to read their stories once more, this time reading more slowly and paying attention to details.
- When students have finished reading, have them do the Complete the Sentences exercise as you circulate among the groups.

Working in the expert groups

- Refer students to their responses on the board and ask each expert group to create a list of questions it could answer with the missing information. Do not ask for answers!
- Check each group's questions before asking individual students to write the questions on the board. If nobody thinks of the question "What does the title mean?" add this question to the board list.
- Ask students to consider what they could do in order to obtain the missing information. If students have done the introductory Jigsaw Word Puzzle activity, remind them of how they shared their clues in order to discover the hidden word. If students don't suggest it themselves, suggest regrouping in Jigsaw groups.
- Have students prepare for their *oral* information-sharing by highlighting or underlining the main points of their readings. Circulate among the groups, making sure students have selected the main points and can speak about them without referring to their printed texts. Allow students to rehearse aloud and assist one another with pronunciation and other problems.

Information-sharing in the Jigsaw groups

- When all students are ready to share their information, have them regroup in their Jigsaw groups.

- Instruct students to take turns sharing their information, beginning with the student who has the A reading. Emphasize the use of the questions on the board as a guide to group discussion.

Directed discussion

Write the following questions on the board for students to discuss in their Jigsaw groups:

1. Did the driver do the right thing?
2. What instructions do you think the general manager should give drivers?
3. Is it important to always follow "the letter of the law?" Why or why not?

Quiz

- Ask each group to indicate when they feel ready to take a quiz. Emphasize the quiz as an independent activity to be done by each student separately. The questions are based on the information in *all* of the readings and on the content of the group discussion.
- Mark the quizzes for comprehension and reasoning only. (Save any grammar and spelling errors for a later grammar lesson!)

Cooperative Skills Development ("Working in Groups," p. 59)

- After returning the quizzes, instruct the Jigsaw groups to discuss these questions for an oral report to the class:
  How can we improve our group's mark on the quiz?
  How can we make sure that everyone in our group understands one another?
  What do our best teachers do to explain something or to help us to understand?
  What responsibility do we have as listeners?
- Record and post somewhere in the classroom students' answers to these questions and encourage students to refer to their responses regularly as a reminder of effective strategies and attitudes to employ in class.
- Have students discuss and complete the cooperative skills sheet "Working in Groups."
- From students' responses, compile a list of useful "gambits" for specific functions and interactions. Post the list somewhere in the classroom for student reference.

Follow-Up

- Using the content of "The Letter of the Law," have students compose a letter from the boy's father to the general manager of the Springfield Metropolitan Transportation Company (SMTC). Have the father explain what happened to his son, his own feelings about the matter, and demand some action. Show students how to set up a formal letter if they are unfamiliar with the appropriate format.

- Have students in pairs exchange letters, and have each student answer the father from the viewpoint of the general manager.

Jigsaw Activity 2: Heart Victim Can't Stay

Synopsis

A young man from Guyana seeks permission to stay in the United States for a heart operation. Immigration officials have refused him an extension of his visitor's visa.

Roles and Reading Levels

A	low intermediate	Raju Harilal, the heart victim
B	low intermediate	Janice Lundgren, an immigration officer
C	intermediate	Shamila Harilal, Raju's wife
D	intermediate	Dr. Olivia Fernandez, Raju's surgeon

Preparation

- Duplicate sets of the "Heart Victim Can't Stay" reading (A, B, C, D) and the accompanying exercise sheets (pp. 60–72), for each Jigsaw group, and copies of the quiz (p. 76) and the cooperative skills sheets "Working in Jigsaw Groups" (p. 77) and "Making a Presentation" (p. 78) for each student.
- Divide the students into their expert groups.

Procedure

Pre-reading

- Write the title of the reading on the chalkboard. Then tell students that the story is about a man who has two big problems and ask "What are the two problems?"
- Accept all student guesses without commenting on their accuracy. Students will confirm or revise their guesses as they read.
- Encourage questions about the title of the reading, but don't answer them. Write the questions on the board for student reference.
- Distribute the readings—A, B, C, or D—to each expert group.

Reading with a purpose

- Allow students no more than one minute to skim their texts to find out if their guesses were correct and to see if they can answer any of the board questions.
- Discuss the students' answers (main idea only: heart problem/immigration problem).

Reading for details

- Write these questions on the board to guide students in a second reading of their texts. "What's wrong with his heart? Why can't he stay?" (Answers: He has a mitral valve problem; his visa has expired.)

Working in the expert groups/Reading skills exercises

- As in "The Letter of the Law," encourage students to highlight or underline the important points of their readings and to rehearse the information with one another.

- Guide students through the reading skills exercises (True, False, or ? and Find the Words), circulating among the groups to answer questions. Consult the Answer Key for "Heart Victim Can't Stay" (p. 151) to confirm answers.
- For the Think About It exercise, ask each expert group to think up and write down four or five questions about their own reading. These questions form the basis of a mini-quiz to be administered later by the experts following their individual Jigsaw group presentations.
- Regroup students in their Jigsaw groups.

Information-sharing in the Jigsaw groups
- As in "The Letter of the Law," students take turns sharing the information from their readings.
- Each student then administers and collects the "mini-quiz" based on the Think About It questions asked in the expert groups and discusses any problems before the next student shares his or her information.

Vocabulary development in the Jigsaw groups

On the board write a list of key words and idioms found in the "Heart Victim Can't Stay" readings. A sample list might look like this:

Key Words
- victim
- immigrate/immigrant/immigration
- apply/applicant/application
- status (marital; in United States)
- medical facilities/treatment/attention
- admit/admission
- permit/permission
- extend/extension
- genuine
- spouse
- sponsor
- patient

Idioms
- send me to my grave
- follow/stick to the letter of the law
- interpret the law with discretion
- consider the case/the circumstances/both sides of the question
- they are determined
- they are not convinced
- set up house/home together

- Encourage students in their Jigsaw groups to share what they know about the vocabulary. Invite the entire class to give examples of how the vocabulary was used in the readings.

Directed discussion
- Have students in their Jigsaw groups pretend they are members of an immigration review committee. Their task is to consider all of the information presented in order to make a recommendation to the Immigration and Naturalization Service (INS). Will the committee advise the INS to follow the letter of the law or to interpret the law with discretion?
- Have each group report its decision to the class.

Quiz

- Distribute the quizzes and accept all well-reasoned answers.
- Mark the quizzes for comprehension and reasoning only.

Follow-Up

- Have students write a memo to the INS making a recommendation based on the committee's deliberations. The memo should present both points of view—the immigration officer's and Raju's—but recommend either to uphold the officer's decision or to allow Raju an extension of his visa. Students can then write a letter from the INS to Raju giving the final decision.
- Assign individual students short research reports on some key facts about the U.S. government and the responsibilities of specific government departments. Have students prepare their questions ahead of time and report back to the class.
- Send students to do a survey to find out how many people in the school know the name of the president, the vice-president, the secretary of state, the governor, the capital of the United States, the state capital, and so on. Again, have students prepare their questions in advance and report back either in writing or orally, using charts or graphs as part of their presentations.

Cooperative Skills Development ("Working in Jigsaw Groups" p. 77; "Making Presentations" p. 78)

- Distribute the evaluation sheet "Working in Jigsaw Groups" so that students can evaluate the Jigsaw approach. From the responses, you will know who is still uncomfortable with cooperative group activity or with the oral aspects of the work. Allow students to work individually on subsequent Jigsaw activities if they wish, but explain that they must still take the same quiz as everyone else. (Since these students will have to complete four times as much material, resistance to this approach should disappear rapidly!)
- Based on your own observations as well as on the students' evaluations, make any necessary changes in the composition of the Jigsaw groups at this point.
- Ask the groups to discuss the questions on the cooperative skills sheet "Making Presentations." Point out the need to use gerunds in completing the sheet.
- Have students discuss which of the strategies listed on the skills sheet they can employ in their own presentations.

Jigsaw Activity 3: Industrial Accident

Synopsis

A serious accident has occurred in the furnace room at the Adams Metal Company. How did it happen? Who is to blame?

Roles and Reading Levels

A	low intermediate	Daniel Vretanos, the injured furnace operator
B	intermediate	Leroy Beckford, the workers' union official sent to investigate the accident
C	low intermediate	Patricia Kowalski, safety engineer at Adams Metal Company
D	intermediate	Vinh-Hoang Ly, the injured man's supervisor

Preparation

- Duplicate sets of the "Industrial Accident" readings (A, B, C, D) and the accompanying exercise sheets (pp. 79–93) for each Jigsaw group, and copies of the quiz (p. 98) and the cooperative skills sheet "Managing and Expressing Disagreement" (p. 99) for each student.
- Divide students into their expert groups.
- Distribute the readings—A, B, C, or D—to each expert group.

Procedure

Pre-reading

- Direct students to look at the first page of their readings and to answer this question: "What is this reading about?" Have students consider how far they had to read to obtain an answer.
- Ask students to look at the diagram that accompanies each reading and to discuss this question in their expert groups: "What do you think happened?"

Reading with a purpose

Have students skim their readings to find out if the answer to the "what happened?" question is in their texts.

Reading for details

- Ask students to reread their texts more slowly, paying more attention to details.
- Have students look for information that will help them decide who is to blame for the accident.

Working in the expert groups/Reading skills exercises

Guide students through the exercises as suggested on pp. 23–24 and consult the Answer Key (pp.151–152) for "Industrial Accident," as necessary.

Information-sharing/Directed discussion in the Jigsaw groups

- Have students regroup in their Jigsaw groups and ask them to compare the information from the four readings to decide on the probable cause of the accident and to find out who, if anyone, is to blame.
- Instruct each group to make some recommendations to the Adams Metal Company on what it and its workers should do to prevent future accidents.

Vocabulary development in the Jigsaw groups

Create a list of key words and idioms drawn from the four "Industrial Accident" readings. Refer to p. 24 for a sample list. Write the list of words and phrases on the board.

Quiz

- Distribute the quizzes and accept all well-reasoned answers.
- Mark the quizzes for comprehension and reasoning only.

Follow-Up

- Get some information booklets on industrial safety or insurance from local government agencies. Have students practice looking for specific information that might apply to the injured worker in the reading.
- Get some sample insurance claim forms and information from a local insurance agent and have students practice filling them out on behalf of "Daniel Vretanos." Students will need to invent information about Vretanos' family life and financial situation: number of dependents, weekly wage, and so on.

Cooperative Skills Development ("Managing and Expressing Disagreement," p. 99)

- Distribute the cooperative skills sheet "Managing and Expressing Disagreement" and review the directions.
- Explain that the skills sheet will help students keep an open mind until they have all of the facts. It will also help students express disagreement effectively but politely without terminating the discussion.

Jigsaw Activity 4: Saving the Biramichi River

Synopsis

The salmon in the Biramichi River are disappearing. Why? Is pollution the major cause? What are the sources of pollution? Are there any solutions to the problem?

Roles and Reading Levels

A	low intermediate	experts from the U.S. Department of Commerce, Bureau of Commercial Fisheries
B	intermediate	the Biramichi Fishing Cooperative
C	intermediate	a consultant hired by the local Chamber of Commerce
D	low intermediate	the Biramichi Chemical Company

Preparation

- Duplicate sets of the "Saving the Biramichi River" readings (A, B, C, D) and the accompanying exercise sheets (pp. 101–124) for each Jigsaw group, and copies of the quiz (p. 125) and the personal evaluation sheet "Working in Groups" (p. 126) for each student.

- Divide students into their expert groups.
- Distribute copies of the readings—A, B, C, or D— to each expert group.

Procedure

Pre-reading

- Direct students' attention to the illustration on the first page of the reading. Ask students these questions: "How do you think the things in this picture are related to each other? How are they related to the title of the reading?"
- Encourage students to guess about the contents of the reading from the illustration and the title.

Reading with a purpose

Have students skim their texts to confirm or revise their predictions.

Reading for details

Ask students to reread their texts, focusing on these questions: "What are some of the causes of the problem? What could be some solutions?"

Working in the expert groups/Reading skills exercises

Guide students through the exercises as suggested on pp. 23–24 and consult the Answer Key (pp. 152–153) for "Saving the Biramichi River," as necessary.

Information-sharing in the Jigsaw groups

Regroup students in their Jigsaw groups and have them compare the information and opinions in the four different readings.

Vocabulary development

Create a list of key words and idioms drawn from the four "Saving the Biramichi River" readings. Refer to p. 24 for a sample list. Write your list of words and phrases on the board.

Directed discussion in the Jigsaw groups

Focus students' discussion on these questions: "What are the causes of the problem? What are the best solutions? Is it possible to satisfy everybody?"

Quiz

- Distribute the quizzes and accept all well-reasoned answers.
- Mark the quizzes for comprehension and reasoning only.

Follow-Up

- Have students write their own recommendations from the point of view of the local residents, the workers in the chemical plant, the town government, or an environmental protection group. Before outlining their recommendations, students will need to ask other Jigsaw group members for information regarding the symptoms and causes of the problem.

- Collect, or have your students collect, different newspaper articles that discuss the various kinds and sources of pollution. Clip off the newspaper headlines and have students match the headlines to the appropriate articles. Then show students how to find the *who/what* of a newspaper article in the headline, the *who/what/when/where* in the first paragraph, and the *how/why* in later paragraphs.
- Have students select one of the newspaper articles from which to summarize and paraphrase for the class the *who/what/when/where/how/why*, either orally or in writing. From the classroom presentations or readings, students can draw up lists or charts to categorize kinds of pollution and their sources. (Find other articles on the hazards and consequences of pollution, as well as its solutions. Consult the science department of your school, your resource librarian, available middle and high school environmental science texts, and environmental groups if you wish to develop this activity into a major topic of study and research.)
- Using information from the readings and other sources, have students practice writing statements of cause and effect (adverbial clauses) as follows:
  Acid rain is caused by ____________________
  As a result of acid rain, ____________________
  Lake George is so polluted that ____________________
  If we continue to pollute the environment, ____________________
  Unless we clean up the lakes, ____________________

Cooperative Skills Development ("Working in Groups," p. 126)

- Distribute copies of the personal evaluation sheet "Working in Groups" and review the directions.
- Explain to students that the evaluation sheet will remind them of their roles and responsibilities as cooperative group members. Students should decide whether this self-evaluation is to be private, shared with the teacher only, or shared with the group.

Jigsaw Activity 5: Who Discovered America?

Synopsis

Credit for the discovery of America is in dispute. Four points of view are presented.

Roles and Reading Levels

A	intermediate	Ancient stories from northern Europe claim the Vikings (Leif Ericsson) discovered America.
B	low intermediate	A British expert claims that John the Skillful, a Welsh sailor, discovered America.
C	intermediate	Some experts say the first people in America came by foot across the Bering Strait.

D low intermediate Many people believe that an Italian, named Christopher Columbus, discovered America.

Preparation

- Duplicate sets of the "Who Discovered America?" readings (A, B, C, D) and the accompanying exercise sheets (pp. 127–147) for each Jigsaw group and copies of the quiz (pp. 148–150) for each student. You might also want to duplicate individual student copies of the personal evaluation sheet "Working in Groups" (p. 126).
- Bring to class at least one globe and copies of a two-dimensional world map, labels removed, one per student.
- Begin this activity with the entire class.

Procedure

Warm-Up

- Distribute the world maps and instruct students to locate and label the continents and oceans. (List them on the board if necessary.)
- Discuss the locations and relationships of places on the globe, emphasizing directions (east/north/south/west of), comparisons (bigger/farther north than), and prepositional phrases (near to, along the coast of, across from).
- Have students compare the globe to their flat two-dimensional maps and discuss the placement of the continents and countries. Ask students "Which continents or countries are placed in the center of the map? If you were a mapmaker in Asia or Australia, how would you place the continents on the map?"
- Have students consider and describe different routes to Asia from Europe, from Europe to America, and to America from Europe, travelling by sea or over land.

Pre-reading

- Divide the students into their expert groups and distribute the readings—A, B, C, or D—to each group.
- Have students compare the map in their Jigsaw reading to the globe in order to determine the perspective from which their map was drawn. Explain to students that their map looks down over the North Pole and has a very different perspective from that of a regular map.

Reading with a purpose

- Ask students to look at the title of the reading and to make some guesses about the answer to the question it asks (Who Discovered America?).
- Direct students to skim their readings to see if any of their guesses are confirmed.

Reading for details

Write the following questions on the board and have students reread their texts more slowly for the answers: When did this person/these people come to America? How did they come to America? Why did they come?

Working in the expert groups/Reading skills exercises

Guide students through the exercises as suggested on pp. 23–24 and consult the Answer Key (pp. 153–154) for "Who Discovered America?" as necessary.

Information-sharing in the Jigsaw groups

Regroup students in their Jigsaw groups and have them compare the information and opinions in the four different readings.

Vocabulary development

- Write the following list of words on the board and have students work cooperatively to figure out the meaning of those words not familiar to everyone in the group. (To make the task easier, create a matching exercise in which students match the word to its definition.)

schol**ar**	archeolog**ist**	marin**er**	expert
anthropolog**ist**	geograph**er**	navigat**or**	ancest**or**
settl**er**	climatolog**ist**	explor**er**	farm**er**
trad**er**	spons**or**	hunt**er**	sail**or**
food gather**er**	descend**ant**	fish**er** (*not* fisher **men**)	

- Point out the common noun suffixes indicating "a person who . . ." and that the suffixes **–er**, **–ar**, and **–or** indicate "a tool, an instrument, or a machine for . . ." Students can list other words with similar endings.
- Discuss some of the sexist suffixes that are now disappearing from English, such as steward/steward**ess** (flight attendant) and so on.

Directed discussion in the Jigsaw groups

Regroup students in the Jigsaw groups and have them compare their information in answer to these questions: "Who really discovered America? Why do you think Columbus got all the credit? Who wrote the history? Why are the native people called 'Indians'?"

Quiz

- Distribute the quizzes and accept all well-reasoned answers.
- Mark the quizzes for comprehension and reasoning only.

Follow-Up

- Have more advanced students evaluate relevant chapters from their history books to determine from whose perspective the books were written.
- Ask students to write an account of a first encounter between Leif Ericsson's people and the native people of Newfoundland, first from the point of view of the original inhabitants, then from the point of view of the newcomers.

Cooperative Skills Development ("Working in Groups," p. 126)

- If you duplicated copies of the personal evaluation sheet "Working in Groups" (p. 126) distribute them to each student and review the directions.
- Explain to students that the evaluation sheet will remind them of their roles and responsibilities as cooperative group members. Students should decide whether this self-evaluation is to be private, shared with the teacher only, or shared with the group.

References and Resources

Aronson, E. et al. *The Jigsaw Classroom.* Beverly Hills, California, USA: Sage Publications, Inc., 1978. A seminal book introducing the Jigsaw concept and offering many useful suggestions for the teacher.

Calderon, M. et al. "Effects of Bilingual Cooperative Integrated Reading and Composition on Students Transitioning from Spanish to English Reading," in *Report No. 10.* Center for Research on the Education of Students Placed at Risk, John Hopkins University and Howard University, USA.

Clarke, J. et al. *Together We Learn: Cooperative Small Group Learning.* Scarborough, Ontario, Canada: Prentice-Hall, 1990. A practical handbook useful to teachers at all grade levels.

Coelho, E. *Learning Together in the Multicultural Classroom.* Markham, Ontario, Canada: Pippin Publishing Limited, 1994. A resource focusing on the implementation of cooperative learning in middle and secondary school classrooms where some or all of the students are learning the language of instruction.

Cohen, E. *Restructuring the Classroom: Conditions for Productive Small Groups.* Review of Educational Research, 1994, No. 64, pp. 1-35. Though not ESL specific, this is well-respected for its practicality and in-depth knowledge.

Cohen, E. *Designing Groupwork: Strategies for the Heterogeneous Classroom.* New York, NY, USA: Teachers College Press, 1986. A book dealing with "status problems" in classrooms where students of many different backgrounds, including recent immigrants, are learning together. Provides guidance on the development of activities that build students' individual strengths in order to promote effective group work.

Davidson, N. and Worsham, T. (eds). *Enhancing Thinking Through Cooperative Learning.* New York, NY, USA: Teachers College Press, 1992. Not specifically about ESL, but filled with interesting perspectives and some adaptable ideas. See, for example, Hilt's chapter titled "The World of Work Connection."

Edge, J. *Essentials of English Language Teaching.* Harlow, Essex, U.K.: Longman, 1993. A book featuring useful information on rationale and techniques for group work.

Erickson, T. et al. *Get It Together: Math Problems for Groups.* Berkeley, California, USA: Regents of the University of California, 1989. Materials for cooperative group learning in math, grades 4-12. Includes a good introduction for the teacher and reproducible clue cards for distribution to students. One of several curriculum resource books from the "Equals" program at the Lawrence Hall of Science, Berkeley—a program of staff and curriculum development designed to promote the equitable participation of minorities and females in mathematics and science. For more information, contact: EQUALS, Lawrence Hall of Science, University of California, Berkeley, California, USA 94720-5220.

Holt, D.D. (ed). *Cooperative Learning: A Reponse to Linguistic and Cultural Diversity.* Washington, DC, USA: Center for Applied Linguistics, 1993. Especially see the chapter by M. McGroaty, "Cooperative Learning and Second Language Acquisition."

Jacobs, G.M. and Ball, J. "An Investigation of the Structure of Group Activities in ELT Coursebooks," in *English Language Teaching Journal,* 1996, Vol. 50, No. 2, pp. 99-107.

Johnson, D.M. "Grouping Strategies for Second Language Learners," in *Educating Second Language Children: the Whole Child, the Whole Curriculum, the Whole Community.* Cambridge, U.K.: Cambridge University Press, 1994, pp. 183-211. An article suggesting ways of grouping students in ESL and mainstream classes.

Kessler, C. (ed). *Cooperative Language Learning.* Englewood Cliffs, New Jersey, USA: Prentice-Hall, 1992. A collection of articles on how to organize group activities in classrooms that include second language learners.

Kowel, M. and Swain, M. "Using Collaborative Language Production Tasks to Promote Students' Language Awareness," in *Language Awareness,* 1994, Vol. 3, No. 2, pp. 73-93.

Liang, X. et al. "Issues of Cooperative Learning in ESL Classes: A Literature Review," in *TESL Canada Journal,* 1998, Vol. 15, No. 2, pp. 13-23. An up-to-date overview of the field, focusing on the benefits of cooperative learning in second language instruction.

McGroarty, M. "The Benefits of Cooperative Learning Arrangements in Second Language Instruction," *NABE Journal,* Vol. 13, pp. 127-133. An article explaining how cooperative learning benefits second language learners and providing examples of cooperative learning in second language classrooms.

Slavin, R. *Cooperative Learning: Theory, Research, and Practice.* Englewood Cliffs, New Jersey, USA: Prentice-Hall, 1990. A resource offering a helpful overview of how and why cooperative learning works.

Warschauer, M. "Computer Mediated Collaborative Learning: Theory and Practice." *The Modern Language Journal,* 1997, Vol. 81, No. 4, pp. 470-481.

Wenden, A. *Learner Strategies for Learner Autonomy.* London, U.K.: Prentice-Hall International, 1991.

All Sides of the Issue

Activities for Cooperative Jigsaw Groups

Duplicatable Student Materials

Introductory Activity 1
Jigsaw Drawing

Base Picture
Questions

1. What is this a picture of? Where are the people?
   Why do you think so?
2. Who are the people in the picture? What are they doing?
   Why do you think so?
3. What else do you see in the picture?
4. Are things missing from the picture? What are they?
5. Are there any things you can't identify in the picture?
   Can you guess what they might be?
6. What are the two words on the chalkboard? What do they mean? Can you think of any times when you needed to clarify for others or ask others to clarify for you? Can you think of times when you tried to encourage someone else or needed someone to encourage you?

Introductory Activity 1: Jigsaw Drawing

Vocabulary

Directions: Study the words, phrases, and questions below. Then practice using them as you and your group complete the Jigsaw Drawing.

Words and phrases to describe details

teacher
- smiling
- looking forward

student(s)
- speaking
- wearing ______
- with ______

hair
- curly
- wavy
- straight
- long / short

shirt / skirt / pants
- star
- stripes

hands

glasses
- square

clock
- round

calendar
- rectangular

notebook

paper(s)

pens
chalkboard
words
window / windowsill
shelf
table
chairs
wall
flowerpot
shade
sun

Words and phrases to describe locations

in / on / under / next to / near the ______
in front of / behind / in back of the ______
facing toward / left / right / away from ______
upper / over / to the right / to the left of ______
top / bottom

Giving directions

Describe ______
Tell me where / what / how ______
Put a ______
Draw a ______

Questions to clarify information

Draw what?
Draw it where?
Which one?
Which side?
How many?
How big?
How long?
Could you say that again, slowly?
Can you say that another way?
What was the word before / after ______ ?
One more time, okay?
I didn't catch that.
What did you say?
Okay, let me repeat that: You said ______ , right?
Could you spell that?

Introductory Activity 1

Jigsaw Drawing

A

Directions: You and your group have different copies of the same Base Picture. Four details are missing from each copy. Take turns asking about the missing details in your picture by describing their location. Take turns answering questions about the details in your picture by describing how they look. As you work with your group, draw in the missing details on your copy of the picture. *Do not look at the other pictures!*

Introductory Activity 1
Jigsaw Drawing

B

Directions: You and your group have different copies of the same Base Picture. Four details are missing from each copy. Take turns asking about the missing details in your picture by describing their location. Take turns answering questions about the details in your picture by describing how they look. As you work with your group, draw in the missing details on your copy of the picture. *Do not look at the other pictures!*

Introductory Activity 1
Jigsaw Drawing

Directions: You and your group have different copies of the same Base Picture. Four details are missing from each copy. Take turns asking about the missing details in your picture by describing their location. Take turns answering questions about the details in your picture by describing how they look. As you work with your group, draw in the missing details on your copy of the picture. *Do not look at the other pictures!*

Introductory Activity 1

Jigsaw Drawing

D

Directions: You and your group have different copies of the same Base Picture. Four details are missing from each copy. Take turns asking about the missing details in your picture by describing their location. Take turns answering questions about the details in your picture by describing how they look. As you work with your group, draw in the missing details on your copy of the picture. *Do not look at the other pictures!*

Introductory Activity 1
Jigsaw Picture

Master Picture (Answer Key)

Questions

1. What are the students in the picture doing?
   Are they having fun? Why do you think so?
2. What time of day and year is it? What is the weather like?
   How do you know?
3. Does the teacher like flowers? Why do you think so?
4. What words does the teacher want the students to remember?
   Why do you think she wants them to remember those words?
5. How does the classroom in the picture compare to classrooms in your country? Is it very similar or very different?

Introductory Activity 2

Jigsaw Word Puzzle

Directions: Share your clues with your group to discover the hidden word in the puzzle below. *Do not look at each other's puzzles!*

Clues

1. This word begins with **R**.
2. There are three **E**s in this word
3. It's in front of us.
4. We have one in the classroom.
5. This word begins with **G**.
6. This word has two syllables.
7. This word ends with **A**.
8. You write in it.
9. For further study.

The hidden word is ___ ___ ___ ___ ___ ___ ___ ___ ___

Introductory Activity 2
Jigsaw Word Puzzle

B

Directions: Share your clues with your group to discover the hidden word in the puzzle below. *Do not look at each other's puzzles!*

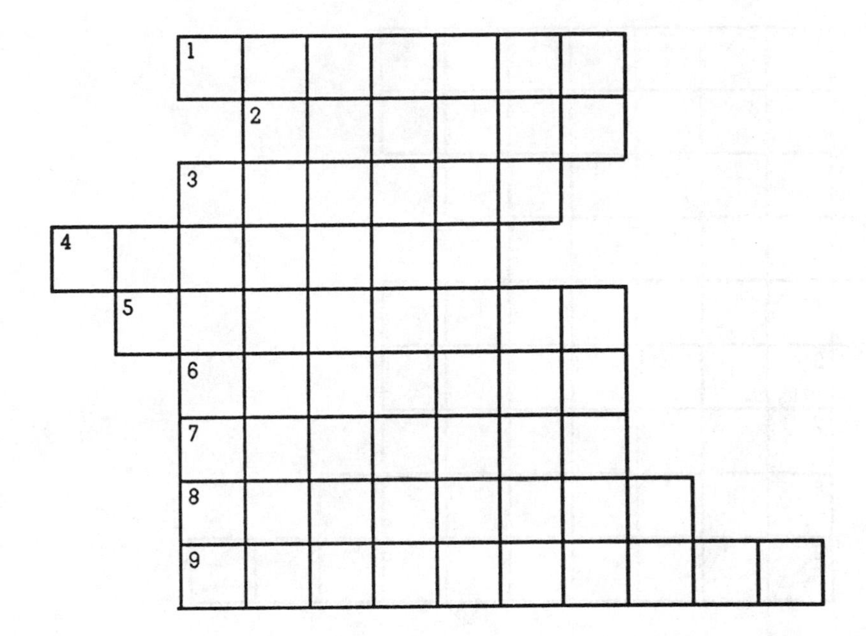

Clues

1. This word ends with . . . **ing**
2. You can't get this at school.
3. This word begins with **F**.
4. He or she is very helpful to us.
5. You do this when you finish your studies.
6. This word begins with **S**.
7. You can get this at school.
8. You bring this to class.
9. This word begins with **U**.

The hidden word is ___ ___ ___ ___ ___ ___ ___ ___ ___

Introductory Activity 2

Jigsaw Word Puzzle

Directions: Share your clues with your group to discover the hidden word in the puzzle below. *Do not look at each other's puzzles!*

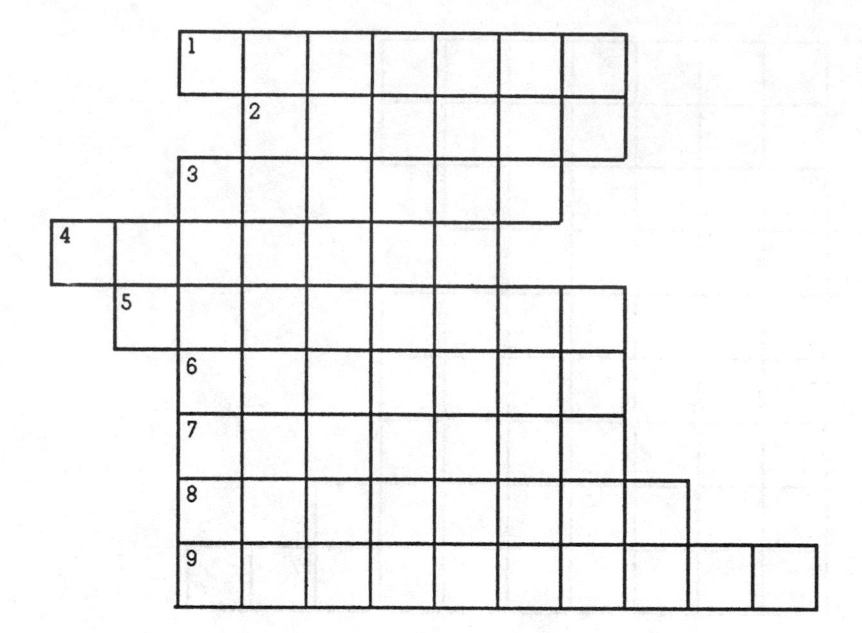

Clues

1. We are doing this.
2. It takes three or four years to get one of these.
3. We can't see it.
4. This word begins with **T**.
5. The last syllable rhymes with **eight.**
6. This word ends with **T**.
7. It's a piece of paper.
8. This word begins with **N**.
9. You can get number 2 there.

The hidden word is ___ ___ ___ ___ ___ ___ ___ ___ ___

Introductory Activity 2
Jigsaw Word Puzzle

Directions: Share your clues with your group to discover the hidden word in the puzzle below. *Do not look at each other's puzzles!*

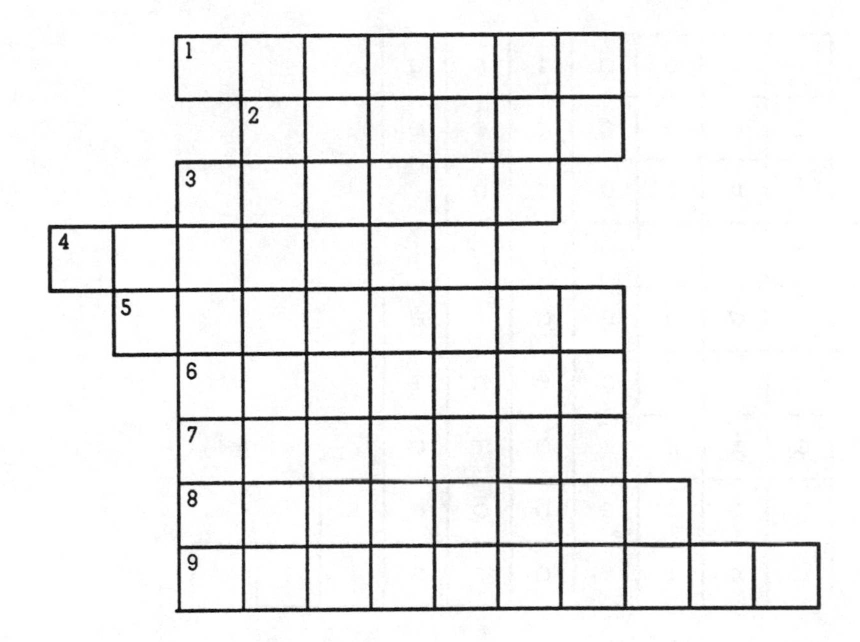

Clues

1. You learn by doing this.
2. You have to study to get this.
3. It's not the past.
4. It's a person.
5. You can do this at school, college, or university.
6. Someone who studies.
7. You have to study for this.
8. This word has three **O**s.
9. You can go there after high school.

The hidden word is __ __ __ __ __ __ __ __ __

Introductory Activity 2
Jigsaw Word Puzzle

Master Puzzle (Answer Key)

		1 r	**e**	a	d	i	n	g			
			2 **d**	e	g	r	e	e			
		3 f	**u**	t	u	r	e				
4 t	e	a	**c**	h	e	r					
	5 g	r	**a**	d	u	a	t	e			
		6 s	**t**	u	d	e	n	t			
		7 d	**i**	p	l	o	m	a			
		8 n	**o**	t	e	b	o	o	k		
		9 u	**n**	i	v	e	r	s	i	t	y

The hidden word is "Education."

Cooperative Skills Sheet: Seeking Clarification

When you work in cooperative groups, the information you have is often incomplete. Sometimes you need to ask for information and sometimes you need to give it. What happens if you don't hear what a person asks or says? What if you don't understand someone or someone doesn't understand you?

Directions: On the lines below, write down some things you can say when you want people to repeat or explain what they have said.

Asking someone to repeat.

1. *Excuse me, would you please repeat that?*
2. __________
3. __________
4. __________
5. __________
6. __________

Asking someone to explain or clarify.

1. *Could you explain that, please?*
2. __________
3. __________
4. __________
5. __________
6. __________

Jigsaw Activity 1

The Letter of the Law

Directions: Look at the picture below. Then read the story on the following page.

Jigsaw Activity 1: The Letter of the Law

Reading

Directions: Read the story below and discuss it with your group.

In Springfield, the public transportation system is operated by the Springfield Metropolitan Transportation Company, known to people in Springfield as the "SMTC."

The SMTC operates on a flat-fare system. That is, every adult pays the same fare, no matter how far he or she is going. There are also other fares: a students' fare, a children's fare, and a senior citizens' fare. You can change from one bus to another, or between the bus and the subway, all for one fare. But you can't stop on the way to do your shopping, or have a cup of coffee, or meet your friend. To do that you must pay another fare.

When you board the bus, or enter the subway station, you pay your fare and take a transfer. The transfer is a slip of paper showing when and where you paid your fare. When changing to a different bus or subway, you show the transfer to the driver or put the transfer in the subway ticket machine. The driver or the machine checks the time to make sure that you haven't been travelling for too long or changed your direction since you started your journey. If the driver or machine finds out you stopped somewhere, you have to pay the fare again.

You must get your transfer at the place where you board the first vehicle. This is the only way that the driver or ticket collection machine can check how long you have been travelling for the same fare. If you don't follow this rule, you will run into problems. That's what happened to the person in the story that some of your classmates have.

Complete the Sentences

Complete the sentences after reading the story.

1. This article is about ______________________________

   ____
2. Buses and subway trains are different kinds of ______________________________.
3. A system where all adults pay the same fare is called a ______________________________ system.
4. You have to take a ______________________________ to show where and when you started your journey.

Jigsaw Activity 1
The Letter of the Law

B

Directions: Look at the picture below. Then read the story on the following page.

Jigsaw Activity 1: The Letter of the Law

Reading

B

Directions: Read the story below and discuss it with your group.

I am a driver for the Springfield Metropolitan Transportation Company. I drive a bus in the afternoons and evenings, along Lawrence Avenue. I have had this job for about two months, and I usually enjoy my work.

Yesterday, my supervisor told me that too many people were travelling for too long on one transfer. He told me that if my passengers want transfers, they must get them when they get on my bus. He said that I should not give a transfer to anyone who asks later, because the rules say they must get transfers at the point where they start their journey.

Yesterday afternoon, at about 4:30 P.M., a young boy got on my bus. He did not take a transfer when he got on. Just as we were coming to the last stop before the bus turns around for the return trip, he asked me for a transfer. I remembered what my supervisor had said, so I refused to give him one. I told him he must take a transfer when he first gets on the bus.

He looked very upset. I felt very bad about it, but I have to do what my supervisor tells me to do. I followed the letter of the law, but I can tell you, I didn't like it.

Complete the Sentences

Complete the sentences after reading the story.

1. This story is about ____

____

2. You have to get your ________________ at the place where you start your journey.
3. The driver ______________________________, but she is not happy about it.

Jigsaw Activity 1

The Letter of the Law

Directions: Look at the picture below. Then read the story on the following page.

Reading

Directions: Read the story below and discuss it with your group.

Yesterday my young son had a terrible experience coming home from his music lesson. It was all the fault of the stupid bus driver.

My son is only nine years old. He has been taking music lessons for two years. We live just over three miles from the music teacher's home. Last year I had to pick him up after his lesson every week because we didn't want him to take the bus alone. However, this year we decided to let him come home on the bus all by himself.

Everything was fine for the first few weeks. He was usually home by five o'clock. Even though he has to take two buses, there are always plenty of buses running at that time of day.

Yesterday, however, he didn't get home until almost 6:00 P.M. It was already dark, and I was going out of my mind with worry. He finally arrived home, exhausted and very upset. He told me that the driver of the first bus had refused to give him a transfer, even though he had asked her for one. She had made him get off the bus without a transfer. Since he didn't have any tickets or extra money for the second bus, he had to walk a mile and a half to get home.

I think this was a most unkind and unreasonable action on the part of the bus driver. I don't know why she did this, but I plan to complain to the general manager of the SMTC. I want an explanation and an apology. This is no way to treat a child!

Complete the Sentences

Complete the sentences after reading the story.

1. This story is about ______________________________
____
2. The child needed a ______________ to get on the second bus.
3. The boy's father thinks the driver was ______________ ______________.
4. He plans to ______________ about her to her employer.

Jigsaw Activity 1

The Letter of the Law

Directions: Look at the picture below. Then read the story on the following page.

Reading

Directions: Read the story below and discuss it with your group.

I am the general manager of the Springfield Metropolitan Transportation Company. My job is to make sure that all our vehicles are running properly, and that we are serving the public well. At the same time, I have to make sure that the passengers and our employees are following certain rules.

Sometimes, if people don't know the rules, they may run into problems on the bus or the subway. We have a flat-fare system in Springfield. We have to make sure that people are using it properly. That's why we have a transfer system.

This morning an angry parent called me about a problem his child had with a driver on one of our buses yesterday. For some reason the child did not get a transfer. The parent said that the driver refused to give his son one. He said that you can't always expect children to follow the letter of the law. He said that we should bend the rules a little bit.

The driver probably obeyed the rules about transfers. Sometimes children or adults want to stop off somewhere. When they get off, they tell the bus driver they forgot to get a transfer. Then the next driver doesn't know what time they really got on the first bus. I will have to ask some questions and get the full story.

Complete the Sentences

Complete the sentences after reading the story.

1. This story is about ____

   ____

2. The general manager will ask the driver for the ____________________
3. He thinks that the driver probably ____________________ the rules.
4. The general manager says he has to make sure that ____________________

   ____

Name ______________________________

Jigsaw Activity 1

The Letter of the Law Quiz

Directions: Work alone to answer the questions below.

True or False?

Write **T** if the statement is true, **F** if the statement is false.

1. ______ Everyone pays the same fare in a flat-rate system.
2. ______ You have to pay again if you change from one bus or subway to another.
3. ______ The driver didn't give the boy a transfer.
4. ______ The boy didn't ask for a transfer.
5. ______ The driver didn't care about the boy.
6. ______ The boy lost his transfer.
7. ______ The boy walked all the way home.
8. ______ The boy's mother called the general manager of the SMTC.
9. ______ "Bend the rules a little" means "Follow the rules exactly."
10. ______ The driver followed the letter of the law.

What Do You Think?

Think about the following questions. Then write your answers on the lines below.

1. Do you think the driver did the right thing? Explain your opinion.

____

____

____

2. If you were the general manager of the SMTC, what would you tell the drivers to do in the future? Why?

____

____

____

Cooperative Skills Sheet: Working in Groups

Groups work better when everyone participates and everyone feels comfortable with the others in the group. Here are some of the things you need to do if you want your group to work well.

Directions: With your group, read the statements and questions below. Then add your own suggestions to 1–4.

1. Make sure everyone has equal turns at speaking.

a. What are some nonhurtful ways to tell someone to finish and allow someone else to speak?

That's very interesting. Maybe we should hear from someone else now

b. What can you say to get a quiet person to participate?

We'd like to hear your ideas on this.

2. Keep on the topic.

What can you say if someone is going off the topic?

Maybe we can talk about that later. Right now, let's discuss...

3. Offer praise and encouragement.

People need to feel that others like what they are saying. If not, they won't speak again. What can you say to show appreciation of other people's ideas?

You explained that really well.

4. Keep a record.

Make sure that someone in the group is making notes of the discussion. You can take turns.

Jigsaw Activity 2

Heart Victim Can't Stay

Directions: Look at the picture below. Then read the story on the following page.

Reading

Directions: Read the story below and discuss it with your group.

1 My name is Raju Harilal. I am from Guyana, and I am 24 years old. I first came to the United States three years ago, to marry my childhood sweetheart, Shamila. She left Guyana eight years ago when her family immigrated to the United States.

2 When we got married, I had a visitor's visa. When it expired, soon after our marriage, I left the United States and returned to Guyana. I stayed in Guyana for three years, but I hoped to join my wife in the United States eventually.

3 Last year I became very sick. I have a serious heart problem. I need an operation to replace a valve in my heart. The doctors in Guyana told me that I need immediate attention, but we don't have the facilities in Guyana for this kind of operation. If I don't get the operation, I will die soon.

4 I contacted the U.S. Consulate in Guyana to get permission to return to the United States, so that I could get the operation to save my life. After ten weeks, I still had not heard from the officials at the Consulate. I was desperate, so I came to the United States as a visitor again. I hoped to get permission here to stay in the United States long enough to have my operation.

5 My visitor's visa expired three weeks ago. I am still here, because the hospital here told me that I can have the operation in two weeks. It is very difficult to get a date for this operation, so I don't want to leave now.

6 Immigration officials here plan to send me back to Guyana tomorrow. They say that I must apply for a new visa from outside the United States. If they send me back home now, they will be sending me to my grave.

7 I beg the Immigration and Naturalization Service (INS) to consider my case, and to interpret the law with discretion, so that I may have a chance to live.

Reading Skills Exercises

True, False, or ?

Write **T** if the statement is true, **F** if it is false, or **?** if you can't find the answer in your reading.

1. ______ He got married three years ago.
2. ______ His wife is a United States citizen.
3. ______ He plans to live in the United States some day.
4. ______ He needs an operation.
5. ______ He came into the country illegally.
6. ______ He will die without the operation.
7. ______ The immigration officials will not let him stay.
8. ______ He wants the INS to help him.

Find the Words

Find words in the reading to match the meanings below. Write the matching word or words on the line next to each meaning.

Paragraph 1:

1. girlfriend ______________________________
2. went to live in another country ______________________________

Paragraph 2:

3. permission to come for a short time ______________________________
4. ended ______________________________
5. after some time ______________________________

Paragraph 3:

6. a kind of medical help ______________________________
7. put in a new one ______________________________
8. the right kind of hospital ______________________________

Paragraph 4:

9. spoke or wrote to ______________________________
10. people who work in a consulate ______________________________
11. I had no hope ______________________________

Continued

A

Reading Skills Exercises *Continued*

Paragraph 6:

12. people who work in the Immigration and Naturalization Service ____________
13. ask for ____________
14. death ____________

Paragraph 7:

15. ask ____________
16. think about my story ____________
17. use the law kindly ____________

Think About It

If you were an INS official, what questions would you want to ask before deciding if Raju Harilal can stay in the United States? Write your questions on the lines below so that you can discuss them later with your Jigsaw group.

1. ____________
2. ____________
3. ____________
4. ____________
5. ____________

Jigsaw Activity 2
Heart Victim Can't Stay

B

Directions: Look at the picture below. Then read the story on the following page.

Jigsaw Activity 2: Heart Victim Can't Stay

B

Reading

Directions: Read the story below and discuss it with your group.

1 My name is Janice Lundgren, and I am an Immigration and Naturalization Service (INS) officer.

2 Last week a young Guyanese man came to see an immigration official. He came with his wife, who is a U.S. citizen. These are the facts of the case.

3 Raju Harilal first came to the United States three years ago on a visitor's visa. While he was here, he got married, but he and his wife did not set up house together. She stayed in the United States when he returned to Guyana.

4 Three months ago Harilal returned, again on a visitor's visa. He brought with him a doctor's letter that says he has a heart problem. He has a date for a heart operation at a hospital for next month, but his visitor's visa expired three weeks ago. Harilal is requesting an extension of his visa to stay in the United States. His wife, Shamila Harilal, also wants to sponsor him as a permanent resident.

5 The INS does not agree to his request for several reasons.

6 First, his operation is not an emergency. He could return to Guyana, and apply for a new visa from there, or wait for permanent resident status.

7 Also, we do not think that his marriage is genuine. It seems that he only got married so that he could apply for permanent resident status as the spouse of a U.S. citizen. His wife did not return to Guyana to live with her husband. In fact, they have never really lived together. They do not have any children. They do not own a house together, or keep a joint bank account. The law permits spouses to sponsor each other when the marriage is genuine, not just to make it easier to enter this country. In the opinion of the Immigration and Naturalization Service, theirs is not a genuine marriage.

8 Another problem is that the United States has a quota system for each country. We can only accept a certain number of people each year from Guyana. This year we already have many more applicants for immigration than we can accept.

9 Finally, we have information that Harilal is a dangerous person, and is a security risk. He was active in certain political groups that use violence. We do not want people like this to come to the United States.

Jigsaw Activity 2: Heart Victim Can't Stay

Reading Skills Exercises

B

True, False, or ?

Write **T** if the statement is true, **F** if it is false, or **?** if you can't find the answer in your reading.

1. ______ Janice Lundgren works for the government of the United States.
2. ______ Her job is to decide who can come to the United States.
3. ______ She has decided that Raju Harilal can stay in the United States.
4. ______ He is very sick.
5. ______ She thinks he is a problem for the United States.
6. ______ She thinks he is honest.
7. ______ He has to return to Guyana.

Find the Words

Find words in the reading to match the meanings below. Write the matching word or words on the line next to each meaning.

Paragraph 3:

1. permission to stay for a short time ______________________________
2. live together as a couple ______________________________

Paragraph 4:

3. a kind of medical help ______________________________
4. ended ______________________________
5. is asking for ______________________________
6. permission to stay longer ______________________________
7. a person who can stay here ______________________________

Paragraph 6:

8. necessary at once ______________________________

Paragraph 7:

9. real or honest ______________________________
10. ask for ______________________________
11. husband or wife ______________________________

Continued

Reading Skills Exercises *Continued*

12. belonging to both of them ______
13. allows ______
14. be responsible for ______

Paragraph 8:

15. allow into the country ______
16. people who ask for permission to come ______

Paragraph 9:

17. safety ______

Think About It

If you were an INS official, what questions would you want to ask before deciding if Raju Harilal can stay in the United States? Write your questions on the lines below so that you can discuss them later with your Jigsaw group.

1. ______
2. ______
3. ______
4. ______
5. ______

Jigsaw Activity 2

Heart Victim Can't Stay

Directions: Look at the picture below. Then read the story on the following page.

Jigsaw Activity 2: Heart Victim Can't Stay

Reading

Directions: Read the story below and discuss it with your group.

1 My name is Shamila Harilal. I am a U.S. citizen. I came here eight years ago when my family immigrated to the United States.

2 Although I was only 13 when I left Guyana, I already had a serious sweetheart. He promised to try to come to the United States to marry me when I was old enough.

3 When I was 18, my sweetheart, Raju Harilal, came to the United States and we got married. He had a visitor's visa, and when it expired he returned to Guyana. We planned that someday he would come to settle here, but in the meantime he had to stay in Guyana to take care of his family. He had been supporting his mother and three brothers and a sister, and he couldn't leave them. I stayed in the United States to finish my studies. I am now in my final year of college.

4 Last year Raju became very sick. His doctors told him that he has a serious heart problem and he needs an operation to replace a valve. Unless he has the operation, he will die. Because they don't have the proper facilities for this operation in Guyana, Raju came to the United States three months ago to have it done at a hospital here.

5 His visa expired three weeks ago, but the hospital says he can have the operation very soon. Now the immigration officials are refusing to give him an extension and say he must leave immediately. Even though my family and I have signed a declaration that we will pay the $20,000 for the operation, the officials have not changed their minds. They are determined to stick to the letter of the law.

6 I haven't slept or eaten in days. How can they be so inhuman? I just want my husband to live. How can they make him leave when we are already married?

7 I beg the Immigration and Naturalization Service to consider my husband's case, and to interpret the law with discretion, so that Raju may have a chance to live.

Reading Skills Exercises

True, False, or ?

Write **T** if the statement is true, **F** if it is false, or **?** if you can't find the answer in your reading.

1. ______ She got married last year.
2. ______ Her husband needs an operation.
3. ______ The operation will save his life.
4. ______ He can pay for the operation himself.
5. ______ He plans to live here after the operation.
6. ______ He came to the United States illegally.
7. ______ The immigration officials have refused to let him stay.

Find the Words

Find words in the reading to match the meanings below. Write the matching word or words on the line next to each meaning.

Paragraph 1:

1. came to live here ______________________

Paragraph 2:

2. boyfriend ______________________

Paragraph 3:

3. ended ______________________
4. live ______________________
5. was responsible for ______________________
6. last ______________________

Paragraph 4:

7. put in a new one ______________________
8. a kind of medical help ______________________
9. the right kind of hospital ______________________

Paragraph 5:

10. people who work in the Immigration and Naturalization Service ______________________
11. permission to stay longer ______________________

Continued

Reading Skills Exercises *Continued*

12. a written promise ____________________
13. do exactly what the law says they should do ____________________

Paragraph 6:

14. unkind ____________________

Paragraph 7:

15. think about it ____________________
16. use the law carefully ____________________

Think About It

If you were an INS official, what questions would you want to ask before deciding if Raju Harilal can stay in the United States? Write your questions on the lines below so that you can discuss them later with your Jigsaw group.

1. ____________________
2. ____________________
3. ____________________
4. ____________________
5. ____________________

Jigsaw Activity 2

Heart Victim Can't Stay

Directions: Look at the picture below. Then read the story on the following page.

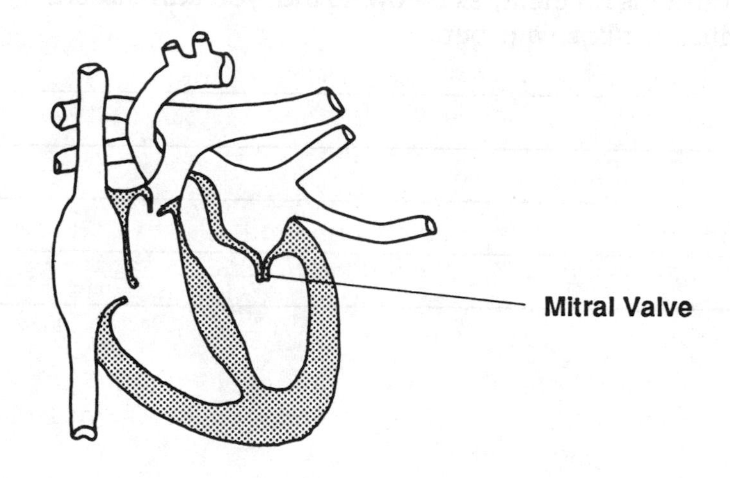

Reading

Directions: Read the story below and discuss it with your group.

1 My name is Olivia Fernandez. I am a cardiovascular surgeon at St. Michael's Hospital.

2 Two weeks ago I examined a patient from Guyana. His name is Raju Harilal, and he is 24 years old. He came to us because his doctors in Guyana advised him that he needed an operation to replace a valve in his heart. Guyana does not have the facilities for such an operation. Harilal came to the United States to get the operation here. He brought with him a letter from his doctor saying that he needed immediate treatment.

3 When I examined Harilal, I confirmed the diagnosis of his doctors in Guyana. He has severe mitral valve disease, and there is a strong possibility of heart failure if the valve is not replaced very soon.

4 This operation is an expensive one. The patient has been informed of the cost, and he knows that he must be responsible for the cost of the operation.

5 The operation is scheduled for two weeks from today. Unfortunately, immigration officials have refused to extend his visitor's visa so that he can have the operation. It is very difficult for us to find a date to schedule this operation. If we don't do it now, Harilal may have to wait six or eight months.

6 In my opinion, Harilal's chances of survival without the operation are very slim. He is likely to die within a few months unless he has the operation. I feel very strongly that the immigration officials should reconsider their decision, and extend his visa so that he may have the operation.

Jigsaw Activity 2: Heart Victim Can't Stay

Reading Skills Exercises

True, False, or ?

Write **T** if the statement is true, **F** if it is false, or **?** if you can't find the answer in your reading.

1. _______ She is a doctor.
2. _______ She is a specialist.
3. _______ She has not examined this patient.
4. _______ Raju Harilal is very sick.
5. _______ He can't pay for the operation.
6. _______ The operation is free.
7. _______ He will die without the operation.
8. _______ He has to leave the United States before the operation.

Find the Words

Find words in the reading to match the meanings below. Write the matching word or words on the line next to each meaning.

Paragraph 1:

1. a kind of doctor _______________________________

Paragraph 2:

2. a sick person _______________________________
3. told him _______________________________
4. put in a new one _______________________________
5. the right kind of hospitals _______________________________

Paragraph 3:

6. found that they were right _______________________________
7. a kind of heart disease _______________________________
8. stopping _______________________________

Paragraph 4:

9. I have told him _______________________________
10. has to pay _______________________________

Continued

Reading Skills Exercises *Continued*

Paragraph 5:

11. give him more time ____________________
12. set a time for ____________________

Paragraph 6:

13. living ____________________
14. small ____________________
15. he will probably ____________________
16. think again ____________________

Think About It

If you were an INS official, what questions would you want to ask before deciding if Raju Harilal can stay in the United States? Write your questions on the lines below so that you can discuss them later with your Jigsaw group.

1. ____________________
2. ____________________
3. ____________________
4. ____________________
5. ____________________

Name ______________________________

Jigsaw Activity 2

Heart Victim Can't Stay Quiz

Directions: Work alone to answer the questions below.

True or False?

Write **T** if the statement is true, **F** if the statement is false.

1. ______ Raju Harilal is a permanent resident of the United States.
2. ______ His wife is a United States citizen.
3. ______ He needs an operation.
4. ______ He has brought money from Guyana to pay for the operation.
5. ______ He wants permission to become a permanent resident.
6. ______ Without the operation, he may die.
7. ______ The Immigration and Naturalization Service (INS) has extended his visa.
8. ______ The INS official is not sure that his marriage is real.
9. ______ The INS official thinks that Harilal is dangerous.
10. ______ The INS says he has to return to Guyana.

What Do You Think?

Should Raju Harilal be allowed to stay in the United States? Give your opinion.

In my opinion, Raju Harilal ______________ be allowed to stay in the United States because ______________________________

____

____

____

____

Cooperative Skills Sheet: Working in Jigsaw Groups

Directions: Work with your group to write answers to the questions below.

1. Why do you think this book is called *All Sides of the Issue*?

2. How is working in Jigsaw groups different from the way you usually work in class?

3. What do you like about working in Jigsaw groups?

4. What don't you like?

Cooperative Skills Sheet: Making a Presentation

When you are working in Jigsaw groups, you have to learn how to present information to the other members of the group so that they understand. What are some of the skills you need to be a good presenter? Think about some of your best teachers. What do they do/did they do to help you understand?

Directions: Work with your group to complete the lists of statements below.

1. Good teachers and presenters help people to understand by:

Writing important words on the chalkboard.

2. Good teachers and presenters try to avoid:

Making people feel stupid.

Jigsaw Activity 3
Industrial Accident

A

Directions: Look at the diagrams below and discuss them with your group.

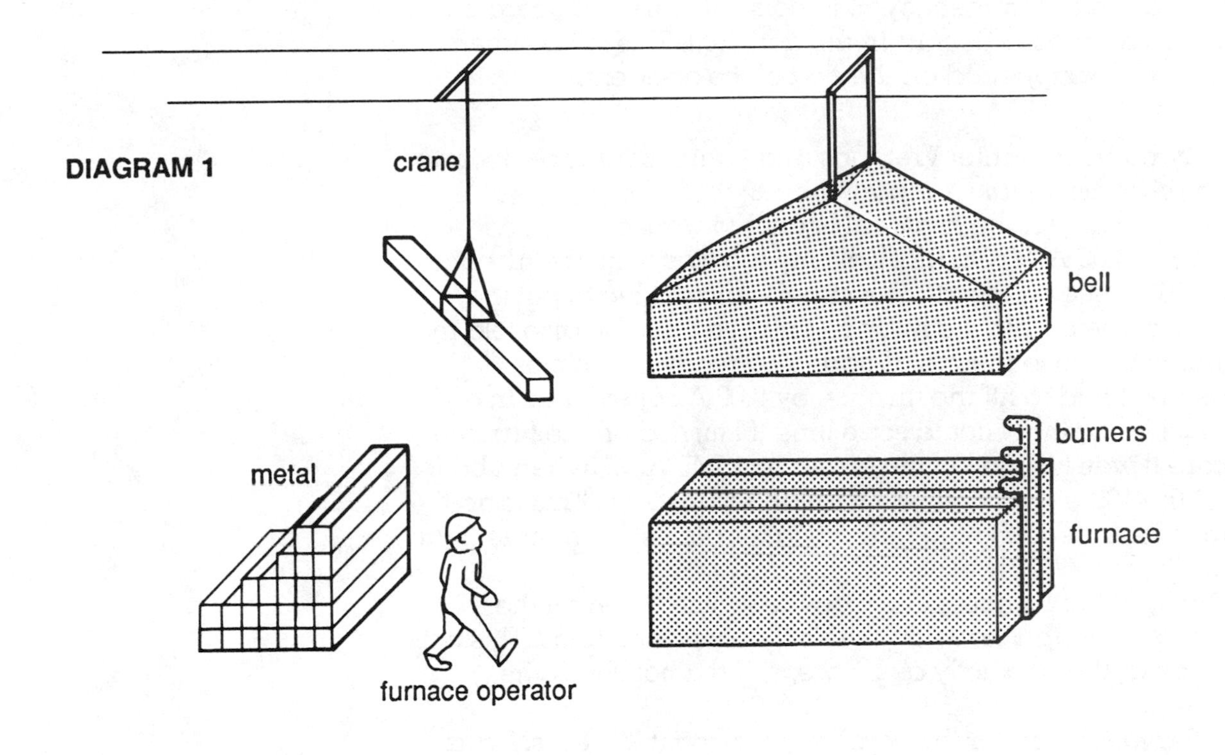

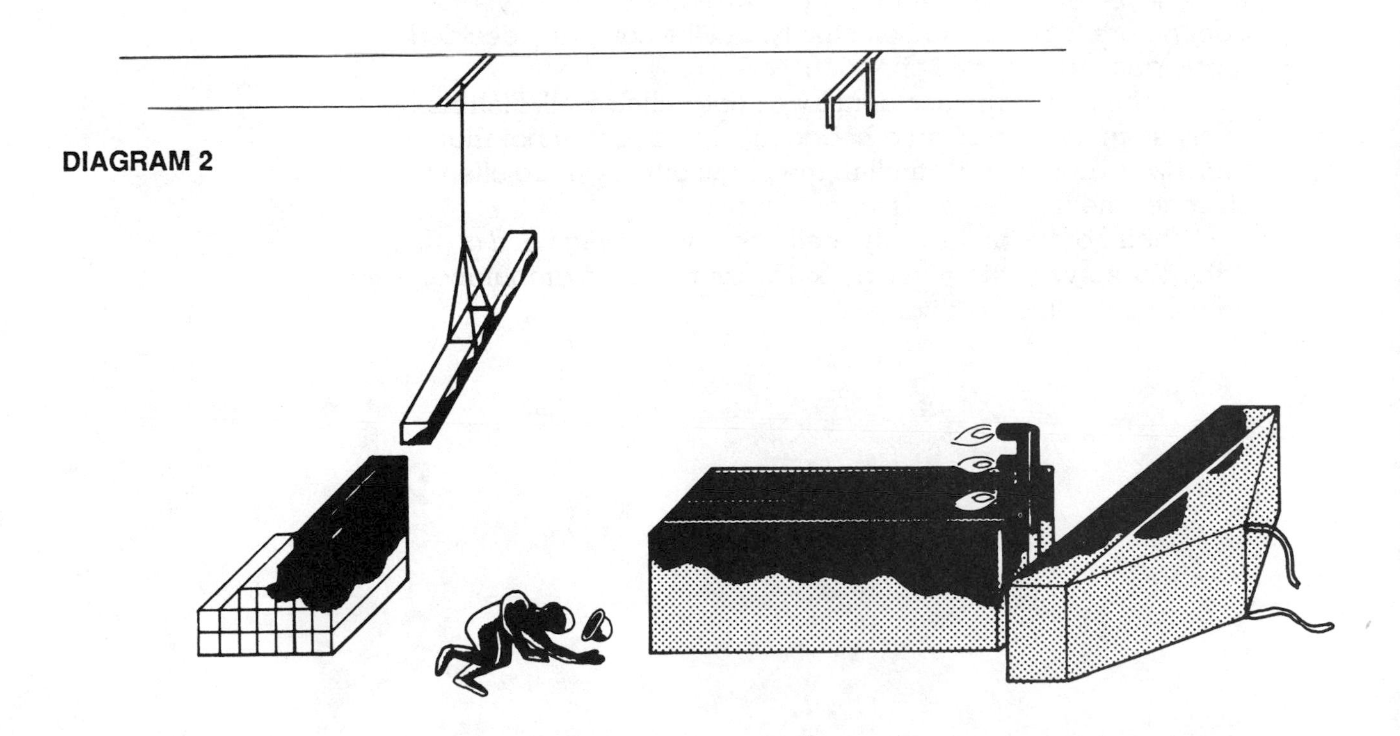

Jigsaw Activity 3: Industrial Accident

Reading

Directions: Read the story below and discuss it with your group.

1 A month ago there was an accident at the Adams Metal Company plant in Steeltown, Illinois. The furnace operator, Daniel Vretanos, was hurt in the accident. This is his statement about what happened on the day of the accident.

2 My name is Daniel Vretanos and I am the furnace operator at the Adams Metal Company plant.

3 On the day of the accident I came to work on time, as usual, at 7:00 A.M. On that day, my job was to fill the furnace with 100 pieces of metal. The supervisor told me to put the pieces of metal into the furnace one at a time. He also told me to hurry because the metal had to be ready as soon as possible. I had to fill the furnace by 8:00 A.M., so I was in a hurry. I knew that I could save time if I turned on the furnace before it was full, so I lit the furnace at 7:45 A.M., when about 75 of the 100 pieces of metal were in the furnace. This is not dangerous, because the furnace takes almost an hour to heat up.

4 To light the furnace, I turn on the switch. Then all the burners light up. I have done this thousands of times. This time I did everything exactly as before, so I did not check the burners.

5 I have worked for the company for about 20 years. I was there when they put in the new gas furnace, about 10 years ago. Before that we used electricity, but the company decided that a gas furnace was cheaper.

6 On the day of the accident I was not feeling well. I felt sick to my stomach and I had a headache. I also remember that there was an unusual smell in the plant, but there are often strange smells in the area where I work.

7 When I brought down the bell, there was a big flash of light. Then everything was dark. I woke up in the ambulance on the way to the hospital.

Reading Skills Exercises

True, False, or ?

Directions: Write **T** if the statement is true, **F** if it is false, or **?** if you can't find the answer in your reading.

1. ______ Daniel Vretanos came late for work.
2. ______ He lit the furnace before it was full.
3. ______ All the burners lit up.
4. ______ There was gas in the air.
5. ______ Nobody else was hurt.

Find the Words

Find words in the reading to match the meanings below. Write the matching word or words on the line next to each meaning.

Paragraph 1:

1. factory ______________________
2. a place for heating metal ______________________
3. worker ______________________

Paragraph 3:

4. the person who tells him what to do ______________________

Paragraph 4:

5. part of the furnace, where the gas comes out ______________________

Paragraph 7:

6. the cover of the furnace ______________________
7. a sudden bright light ______________________
8. a special car that takes people to the hospital ______________________

Jigsaw Activity 3: Industrial Accident

Reading Skills Exercises

Think About It

Directions: With your group, discuss answers to the following questions. Write your answers on the lines below.

1. Why was he in a hurry?

____

____

____

2. Why does the company have a gas furnace?

____

____

____

3. Did the furnace operator make any mistakes? Explain your opinion.

____

____

____

4. Is this a good place to work? How do you know?

   In my opinion, this plant ____________ a good place to work because ____________

____

____

____

____

____

5. What questions would you like to ask about this story before deciding who is to blame for the accident?

____

____

____

____

____

Jigsaw Activity 3
Industrial Accident

B

Directions: Look at the diagrams below and discuss them with your group.

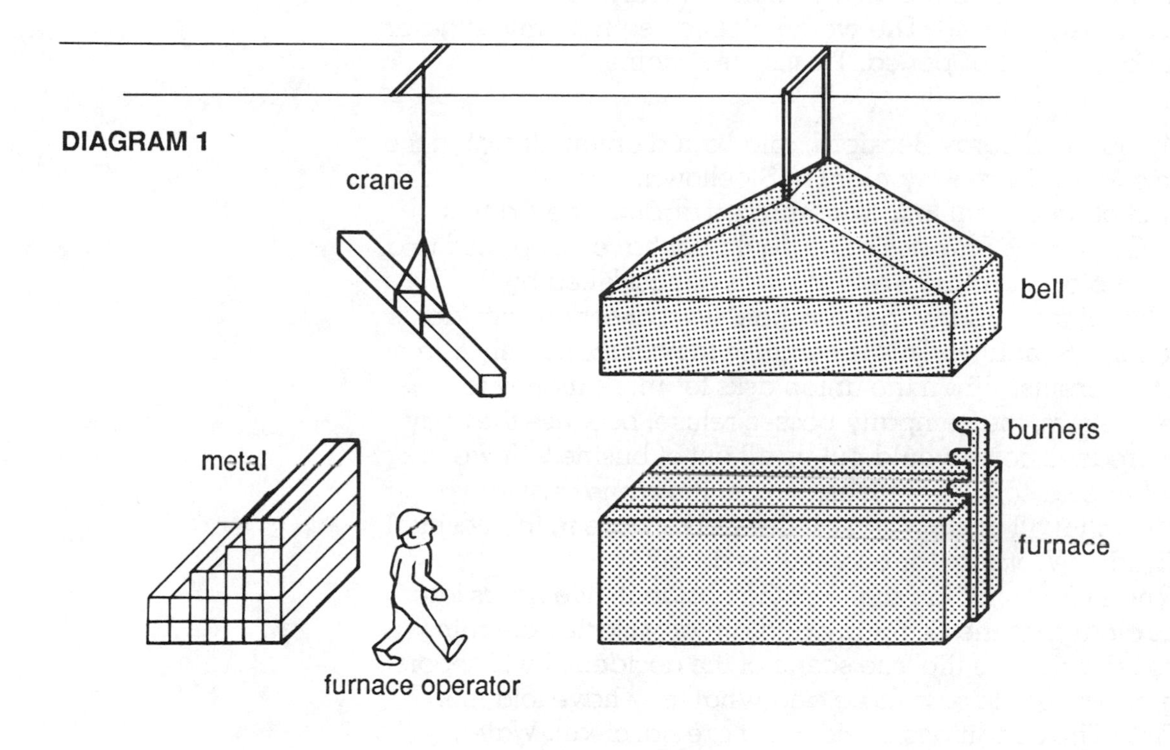

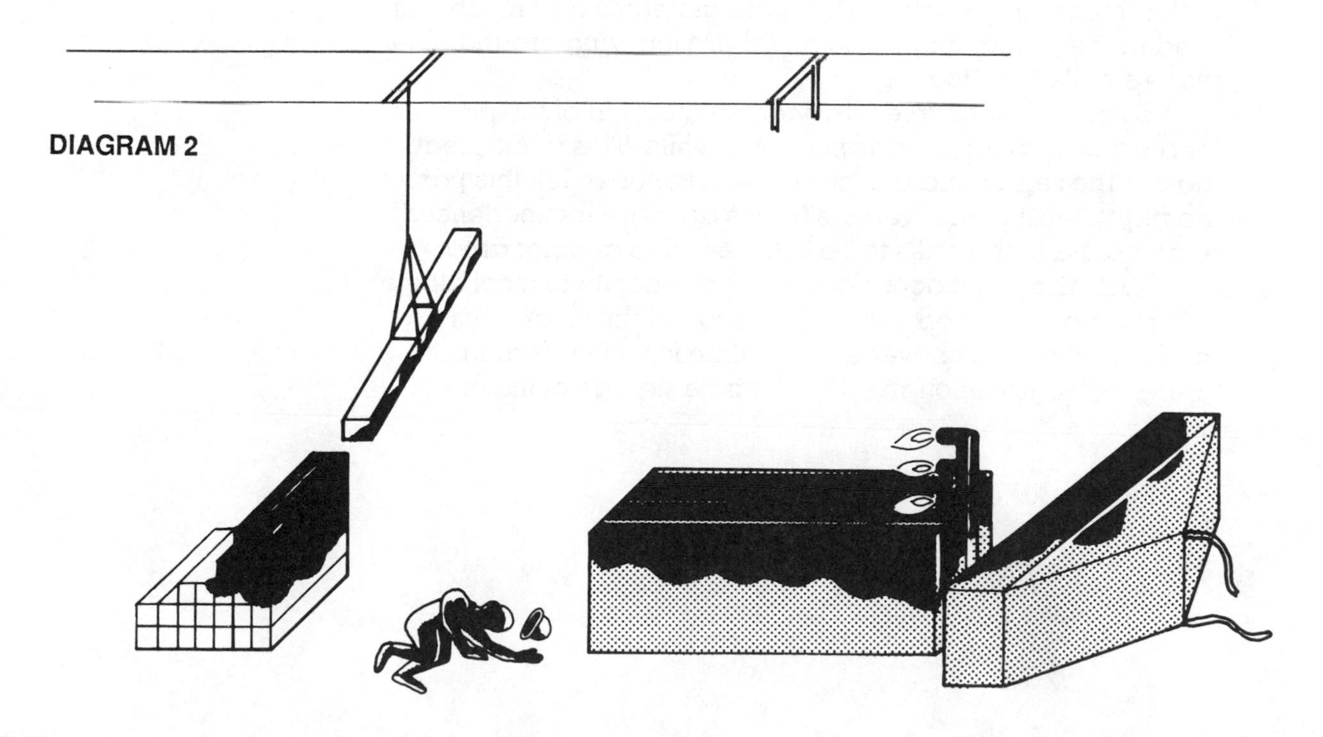

Reading

B

Directions: Read the story below and discuss it with your group.

1 A month ago there was an accident at the Adams Metal Company plant in Steeltown, Illinois. The furnace operator was seriously injured. The workers' union sent an investigator to find out what happened. This is his statement.

2 My name is Leroy Beckford, and I am a union official at the Adams Metal Company plant in Steeltown.

3 First of all, I want to make a protest against the Adams Metal Company. This accident would not have happened in a well-run plant. Brother Vretanos was almost killed by the stupidity of a company that has had several serious accidents in the last 18 months. This is because the company only cares about its profits. When the union asks for more money for more workers, the company bosses refuse, because they say the increased costs would put us all out of business. If we ask for better and safer machines, we get the same answer. Where will it all end? When all the workers are in the hospital, like Brother Vretanos, or one of us is dead?

4 When I first saw the scene of the accident, five hours later, it was clear that the company had already started cleaning up, so I did not see the true scene of the accident. I will report what other people saw there and what they have told me.

5 First: The conditions in the plant are not clean. Water, rusted metal, and garbage from the materials and machines used in the processing of the metal are left lying around. The place smells bad, too.

6 Second: Most people who work in that part of the plant ask for a transfer to another area after a while. This means that most of the senior, more experienced staff have left this part of the plant; most of the workers in this area are inexperienced, or do not have the skills to be transferred to another area.

7 Third: The plant does not have the capacity to meet all the orders unless we work three shifts around the clock. This means that there is never enough time for good cleanup. There is also not enough space for safe storage of materials.

Continued

8 Fourth: The plant is so badly run that everything is a "rush" order. When we are working under this kind of pressure, there is a greater risk of accidents.

9 Fifth: This is the 12th accident that I have investigated at this company in the past 18 months.

10 On behalf of the workers of Local 423-A of the Blacksmiths' Union, and Local 112 of the Machinists' Union, I demand that these steps be taken:

1. The Occupational Safety and Health Administration must investigate this accident and any other accident that happens here.
2. Each shift should get half an hour of paid cleanup time at the end of the shift.
3. The company must invest in new equipment, and in expansion of the plant.
4. All supervisors should take a safety course in accident prevention, at the company's expense.
5. The company should negotiate with the union for a new benefits program to include better life and accident insurance.

Jigsaw Activity 3: Industrial Accident

Reading Skills Exercises

True, False, or ?

Directions: Write **T** if the statement is true, **F** if it is false, or **?** if you can't find the answer in your reading.

1. ______ Leroy Beckford blames the company for the accident.
2. ______ He doesn't work at the plant.
3. ______ He is representing the workers.
4. ______ Daniel Vretanos is his brother.
5. ______ He was called to the scene immediately.
6. ______ He has some ideas for improving the working conditions.

Find the Words

Find words in the reading to match the meanings below. Write the matching word or words on the line next to each meaning.

Paragraph 1:

1. hurt ______________________
2. someone who asks questions ______________________

Paragraph 3:

3. angry complaint ______________________
4. lose our jobs ______________________

Paragraph 5:

5. manufacturing ______________________

Paragraph 6:

6. a change or a move ______________________
7. knowledge or training ______________________

Paragraph 7:

8. is not big enough ______________________
9. length of time people work each day ______________________

Paragraph 8:

10. working too hard, working too fast ______________________
11. possibility ______________________

Continued

Paragraph 10:

12. changes should be made ____________________
13. spend some money on ____________________
14. machines ____________________
15. making it bigger ____________________
16. making sure that accidents can't happen ____________________
17. the company will pay for it ____________________
18. discuss and agree on ____________________
19. when you work, you get money and . . . ____________________

Think About It

Directions: With your group, discuss answers to the following questions. Write your answers on the lines below.

1. What does a union official do?

____
____
____
____

2. Why do you think Leroy Beckford wasn't called immediately?

____
____
____
____

3. Is this a good place to work? How do you know?

In my opinion, this plant ____________ a good place to work because ____________

____
____
____

Continued

Reading Skills Exercises *Continued*

B

4. What do you think the company should do to improve conditions?

5. What questions would you like to ask about this story before deciding who is to blame for the accident?

Jigsaw Activity 3
Industrial Accident

Directions: Look at the diagrams below and discuss them with your group.

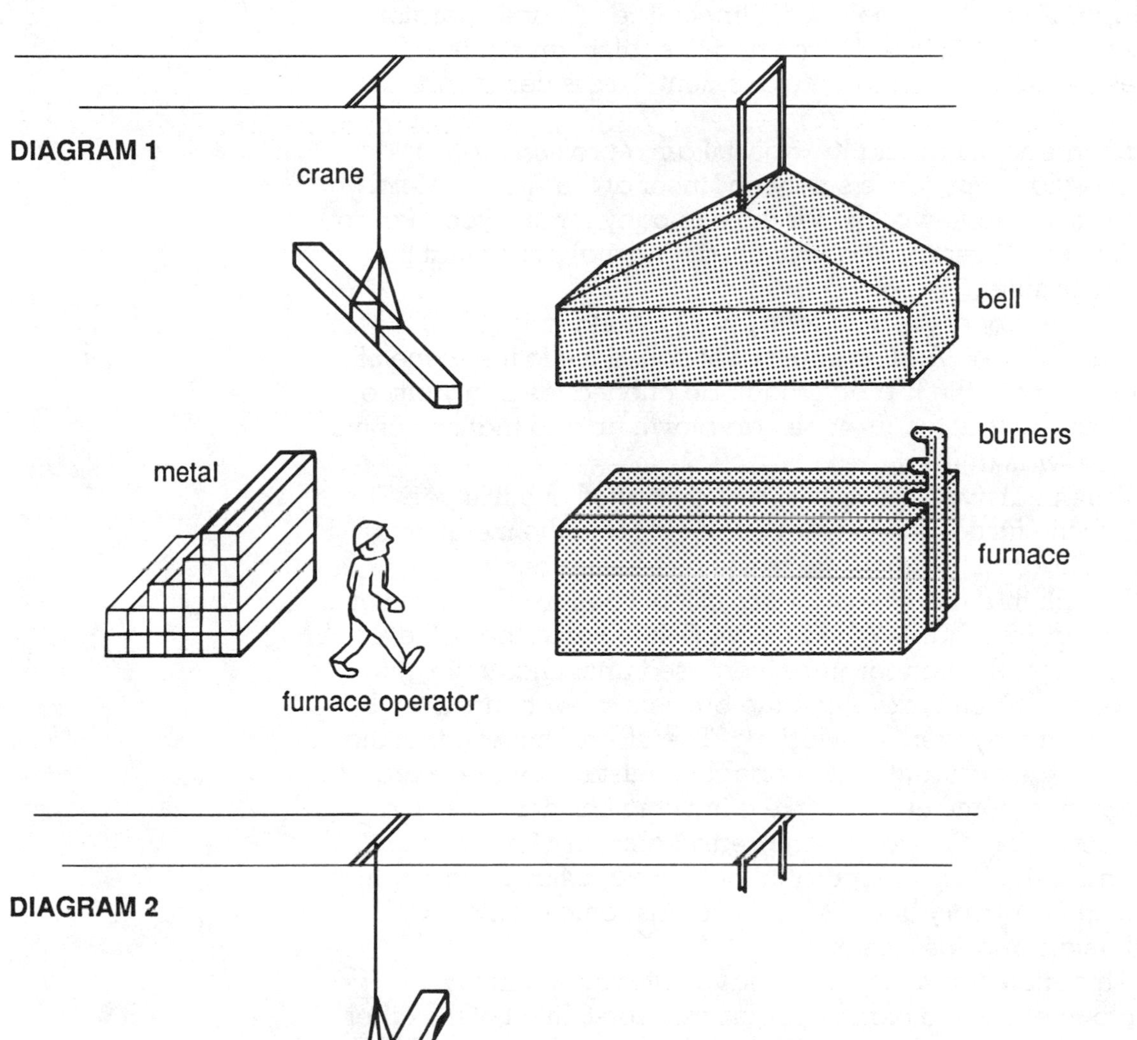

Jigsaw Activity 3: Industrial Accident

Reading

Directions: Read the story below and discuss it with your group.

1 A month ago there was an accident at the Adams Metal Company plant in Steeltown, Illinois. The furnace operator was seriously injured. The company's safety engineer investigated the cause of the accident. This is her report.

2 My name is Patricia Kowalski. I am a professional engineer and my job is safety engineer at the Adams Metal Company. I have worked for the company for one year. Part of my job is to investigate accidents and to make sure that the factory is safe.

3 On the day of the accident, I was in the plant at 8:30 A.M., as usual. At 8:45 A.M., a supervisor called me to the scene of an accident in the furnace room. He phoned me in my office and told me that the furnace had blown up and that one of his workers was injured.

4 When I arrived, there was a strong smell of burnt gas. The bell for the furnace was lying on its side and the metal was black. Diagram 2 shows the scene as I remember it.

5 I think that there was an explosion. I believe that some of the gas did not burn. When the worker lowered the bell over the furnace, the temperature increased until finally the gas exploded. When I examined the burners a few hours later, I found that they were all working. Therefore, I believe that the cause of the accident was probably a mistake by the operator. Sometimes, some of the workers hurry to finish a job so that they can take a longer lunch break. I am sorry for Mr. Vretanos, the furnace operator, but I have noticed that his English is not very good. Maybe he has some problems understanding instructions.

6 This is the tenth accident I have investigated in my employment at the plant; it is also the worst. In all of the other accidents, nobody needed to go to the hospital.

7 I believe that the company is not to blame in this unfortunate accident.

Jigsaw Activity 3: Industrial Accident

Reading Skills Exercises

C

True, False, or ?

Directions: Write **T** if the statement is true, **F** if it is false, or **?** if you can't find the answer in your reading.

1. ______ The safety engineer saw the accident.
2. ______ One worker was hurt.
3. ______ There have been ten accidents this year.
4. ______ This is a dangerous factory.
5. ______ The furnace operator died.
6. ______ The safety engineer blames the furnace operator for the accident.

Find the Words

Find words in the reading to match the meanings below. Write the matching word or words on the line next to each meaning.

Paragraph 1:

1. tried to find out ____________________

Paragraph 3:

2. factory ____________________
3. a place to heat metal ____________________
4. exploded ____________________
5. hurt ____________________

Paragraph 4:

6. the place where the accident happened ____________________

Paragraph 5:

7. became hotter ____________________

Paragraph 7:

8. not responsible for ____________________

Jigsaw Activity 3: Industrial Accident

Reading Skills Exercises

Think About It

Directions: With your group, discuss answers to the following questions. Write your answers on the lines below.

1. How does the safety engineer know there was an explosion?

____

____

____

____

2. How does she think it happened?

____

____

____

____

____

3. Who does she blame for the accident? Why?

She blames _______________ because _______________

____

____

____

4. Is this a good place to work? How do you know?

In my opinion, this plant _______________ a good place to work because _______________

____

____

____

____

____

5. What questions would you like to ask about this story before deciding who is to blame for the accident?

____

____

____

____

____

Jigsaw Activity 3
Industrial Accident

D

Directions: Look at the diagrams below and discuss them with your group.

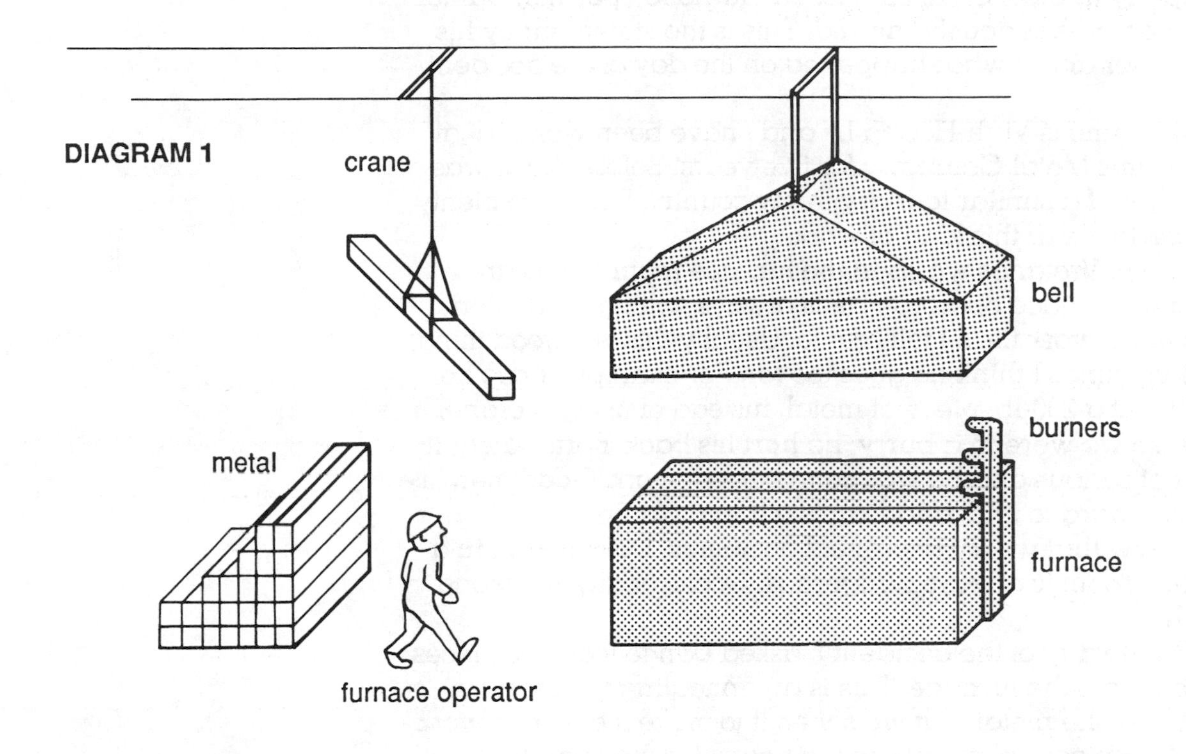

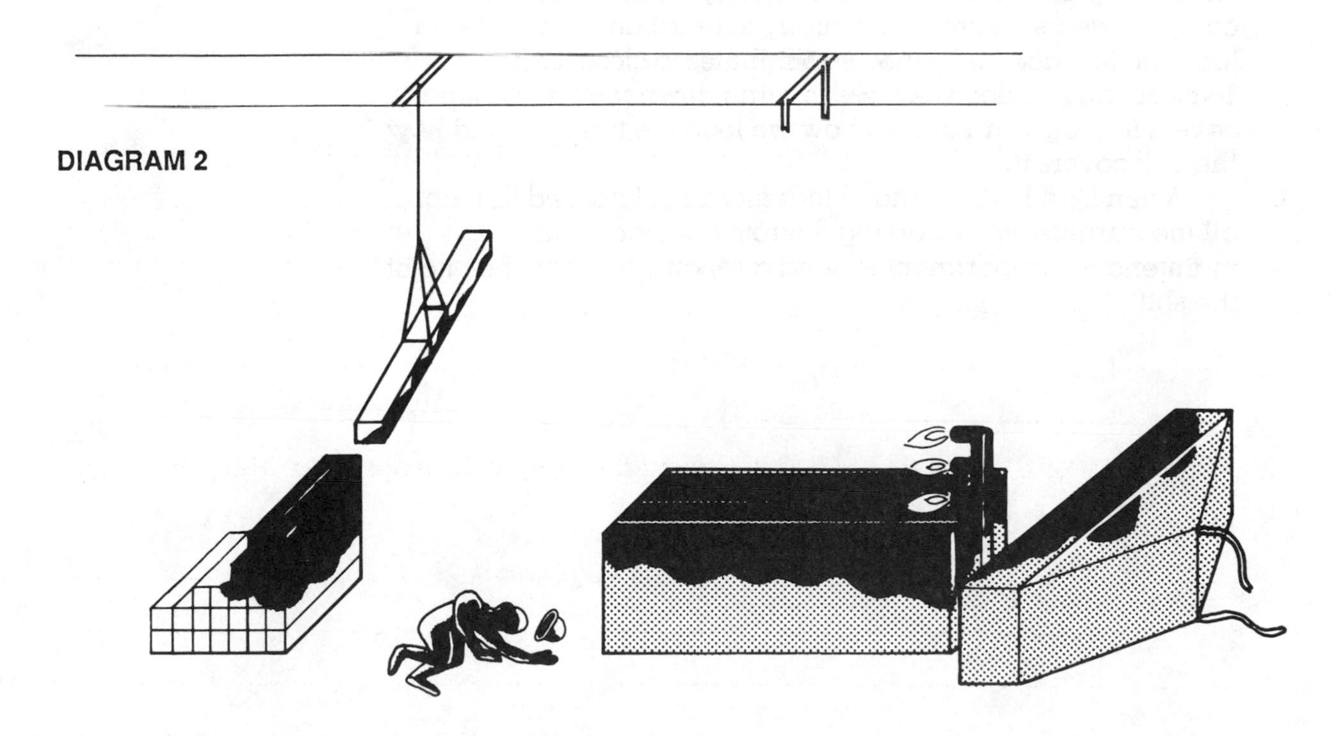

Jigsaw Activity 3: Industrial Accident

Reading

Directions: Read the story below and discuss it with your group.

1 A month ago there was an accident at the Adams Metal Company in Steeltown, Illinois. The furnace operator, Daniel Vretanos, was seriously injured. This is the statement by his supervisor about what happened on the day of the accident.

2 My name is Vinh-Hoang Ly and I have been working at the Adams Metal Company for five years. Before that, I was manager of a similar foundry in my country. So I have plenty of experience in this kind of work.

3 Daniel Vretanos works in the furnace room and is an excellent furnace operator. He is always willing, and often does more work than I tell him to. Usually this is a good thing, but sometimes I think he goes too far. For example, once he tried to lift a 200-lb. piece of metal, instead of using a crane, because we were in a hurry; he hurt his back. Fortunately, it was not serious and he was soon back at work. Good men like Dan are hard to find, and Dan is a friend of mine.

4 I know that we try to prevent accidents, but working in a furnace room is always dangerous. Occasionally, someone gets hurt.

5 On the day of the accident I asked Dan to load 100 pieces of metal into the furnace. This is an annealing furnace; we don't melt the metal, but we soften it to make it easier to work with. The pieces of metal are too heavy for the operator to carry, so we use a crane. It usually takes about 90 minutes to load the furnace, and another 5 minutes to close it and light it. To close the furnace we have to bring down the bell which covers it. Diagram 1 shows how we load the furnace, and how the bell covers it.

6 When Dan lit the furnace that morning, I noticed that not all the burners were working. I wrote a memo for the maintenance department to send a repair person at the end of the shift.

Continued

Reading *Continued*

7 I was about 100 yards away when the furnace exploded. Suddenly there was a loud bang, and when I ran over I saw the bell lying on its side. Dan was lying on the floor and had bad burns on his head, face, and arms. He was unconscious. I covered him with a blanket and called an ambulance. He was still unconscious when the ambulance arrived.

8 Dan was in the hospital for three weeks, and needs plastic surgery to repair the burns on his face and hands. He lost his hair, but it is growing back now. His doctor tells him he needs three or four months of rest before he can return to work.

Reading Skills Exercises

True, False, or ?

Directions: Write **T** if the statement is true, **F** if it is false, or **?** if you can't find the answer in your reading.

1. ______ The furnace operator is a good worker.
2. ______ The furnace operator sometimes makes mistakes.
3. ______ They melt metal in the furnace.
4. ______ They use a gas furnace.
5. ______ There was something wrong with the furnace.
6. ______ The supervisor called the maintenance department to fix it immediately.
7. ______ The furnace operator was killed.

Find the Words

Find words in the reading to match the meanings below.
Write the matching word or words on the line next to each meaning.

Paragraph 1:

1. the person who tells the workers what to do ______________________

Paragraph 2:

2. a factory where people soften metal ______________________

Paragraph 3:

3. happy to work ______________________
4. does too much, tries too hard ______________________
5. a machine for lifting heavy things ______________________

Paragraph 4:

6. keep from happening ______________________
7. sometimes ______________________

Paragraph 6:

8. a written message ______________________
9. the group of workers who fix the machines ______________________
10. a special car that takes people to the hospital ______________________

Continued

Paragraph 8:

11. operations that make the skin look better. ______________________

Think About It

Directions: With your group, discuss answers to the following questions. Write your answers on the lines below.

1. Why does the supervisor talk about Dan's previous injury?

____

____

____

____

2. Did the supervisor make any mistakes? Explain your opinion.

____

____

____

____

3. Is this a good place to work? How do you know?

   In my opinion, this plant ____________ a good place to work because ____________

____

____

____

4. What questions would you like to ask about this story before deciding who is to blame for the accident?

____

____

____

____

Name ______________________________

Jigsaw Activity 3
Industrial Accident Quiz

Directions: Work alone to answer the questions below.

True or False?

Write **T** if the statement is true, **F** if the statement is false.

1. ______ The furnace operator was a new worker at the plant.
2. ______ The furnace operator checked the burners.
3. ______ The furnace operator died in this accident.
4. ______ The supervisor knew there was something wrong with the furnace.
5. ______ The supervisor sent for a repair person right away.
6. ______ The supervisor says the furnace room is a safe place to work.
7. ______ The union official thinks this is a safe plant.
8. ______ The union official wants some changes at the plant.
9. ______ The safety engineer saw the accident.
10. ______ The safety engineer blames the furnace operator for the accident.

What Do You Think?

Write your answers to the following questions.

1. What do you think caused the accident?

____

____

2. Who do you think is to blame for the accident?

I think ____________________ is/are to blame because ____________________

____

____

3. What are some of the problems at this plant?

____

____

4. What do you think the company should do now?

____

____

Cooperative Skills Sheet: Managing and Expressing Disagreement

When you are working in a Jigsaw group, each person has different information on the same topic. Sometimes that information is so different that you may have a very different opinion from other members of the group.

Directions: Read the information and questions below. Then work with your group to add to each list. Follow the examples.

1. **Listen to the information that others have.**
   Information from other people may cause you to change your opinion. What can you say to get someone to explain to you why they have a different opinion?
   I don't understand why you think so. Would you explain your reason?

2. **Disagree politely, giving reasons for your opinion.**
   You may have information that will cause others in your group to reconsider their opinion. What can you say to introduce a disagreement or a different opinion?
   I don't agree with you, because

3. **Reach a compromise.**
   Try to find an opinion that everyone can accept. Maybe everyone has to change his or her mind a little bit. If you have listened to everyone, and everyone has listened to you, you may be able to find an opinion on which everyone can agree. What can you say to try to reach a compromise?
   Let's find the points we agree on.

Continued

Cooperative Skills Sheet:
Managing and Expressing Disagreement *Continued*

4. Agree to disagree.

If it seems impossible for you to reach a compromise maybe you can agree that it is not necessary for everyone to agree this time. Everyone can have a different opinion as long as they can give good reasons for their opinion. What can you say to close the discussion without forcing everyone to accept the same opinion?

I guess we all have to make up our own minds about this.

Jigsaw Activity 4
Saving the Biramichi River

A

Directions: Look at the picture below. How do you think the things in the picture are related to each other? How are they related to the title of the reading?

Jigsaw Activity 4: Saving the Biramichi River

Reading

Directions: Read the story below and discuss it with your group.

1 There are some serious problems in the Biramichi River. Several groups have studied the problems. This is the opinion of the experts from the Bureau of Commercial Fisheries in the U.S. Department of Commerce, which is responsible for the laws about commercial fishing:

2 There is a serious problem with salmon in the Biramichi River. Each year there are fewer fish in the river, and each year the fishers catch fewer fish. If the situation does not improve immediately, there will soon be no salmon in the river.

3 What are the causes of the problem? We can identify three main causes:

- The biggest problem is human sewage which flows from the toilets of the houses and summer vacation homes in the area. The problem is greatest in the summer months, when the weather is hot, and there are more residents in the area. We estimate that the sewage causes 60% of the pollution in the river.
- The second problem is chemical pollution from the four large factories near the river. They pour millions of gallons of polluted water into the river each year. This causes 20% of the problem in the river.
- The third problem is over-fishing. The people who fish for a living in the area are taking too many fish. Each year we set quotas for the number of fish they can take, but each year we find fewer and fewer fish. We estimate that over-fishing is responsible for 20% of the problem.

4 We suggest three solutions to the problem:

- Build new sewage treatment plants to treat the sewage before it gets into the river.
- Stop the factories from pouring polluted water into the river.
- Ban fishing in the river for three years.

Reading Skills Exercises

A

True, False, or ?

Write **T** if the statement is true, **F** if it is false, or **?** if you can't find the answer in your reading.

1. _______ There is a problem in the river.
2. _______ There are not enough fish in the river.
3. _______ The biggest problem is over-fishing.
4. _______ The problem is greatest in the winter.
5. _______ There is a lot of chemical pollution in the water.
6. _______ The chemical pollution comes from the toilets in the area.
7. _______ The pollution is killing the fish.
8. _______ Everyone in the area will be happy to follow the experts' advice.

Find the Words

Find words in the reading to match the meanings below. Write the matching word or words on the line next to each meaning.

Paragraph 2:

1. a kind of fish ______________________________
2. get better ______________________________

Paragraph 3:

3. find ______________________________
4. dirty water from the toilet ______________________________
5. people who live there ______________________________
6. calculate ______________________________
7. dirty, unhealthy water ______________________________
8. taking too many fish ______________________________
9. tell them how many to take ______________________________
10. is the cause of ______________________________

Continued

Reading Skills Exercises *Continued*

Paragraph 4:

11. answers ____________________
12. places where people can clean the water ____________________
13. places where people make things ____________________
14. stop ____________________

Find the Meaning

Find the words on the left in the reading. Then match each word to its meaning by checking (✔) a, b, or c. *Do not use a dictionary!*

Paragraph 1:

1. experts
   a. people who know a lot about a subject
   b. people who teach
   c. people who study

2. commercial
   a. done for pleasure
   b. an advertisement
   c. done for money

Paragraph 3:

3. flows
   a. grows
   b. becomes
   c. moves

4. pour
   a. empty into
   b. turn over
   c. take away

Paragraph 4:

5. to treat the sewage
   a. to pay for
   b. to clean with chemicals
   c. to carry away

Find the Details

List the problems that the Bureau found. Then list the solutions the Bureau suggests.

Problems	Solutions
____________________	____________________
____________________	____________________
____________________	____________________
____________________	____________________

Jigsaw Activity 4: Saving the Biramichi River

Reading Skills Exercises

Think About It

Read the following questions and discuss them with your group. Then write your answers on the lines below.

Who will be unhappy about the solutions that the Bureau of Commercial Fisheries suggests? Why do you think so?

1. I think the ______________________________ will be unhappy because
____
____
____
____
____

2. I think the ______________________________ will be unhappy because
____
____
____
____
____

3. I think the ______________________________ will be unhappy because
____
____
____
____
____

Jigsaw Activity 4

Saving the Biramichi River

B

Directions: Look at the picture below. How do you think the things in the picture are related to each other? How are they related to the title of the reading?

Reading

B

Directions: Read the story below and discuss it with your group.

1 There are some serious problems in the Biramichi River. Several groups have studied the problems, including the Biramichi Fishing Cooperative. The Cooperative represents the opinion of the people who make a living from fishing for salmon in the river. This is the Cooperative's opinion:

2 We represent the 250 families who depend on the Biramichi River for making a living. We and our ancestors have been fishing in the Biramichi for hundreds, perhaps thousands, of years. Our people were the first people here. For many generations, until the coming of the white people, our people were the guardians of the land and the wildlife in the area. Therefore, we have rights to the land and the water, and we claim these rights today. We were here before the Europeans came. We have a traditional right to fish in these waters.

3 Now the U.S. Bureau of Commercial Fisheries and the Bureau of Indian Affairs tell us how to fish, where to fish, when to fish, and how many fish to take. We must listen to people from the city when they make laws about our land and our water. Now the government blames us for the problems in the river, and says we must stop fishing.

4 It is true that there used to be more salmon in the river than there are now. It is true that there are fewer salmon each year, and that each year the salmon are smaller. However, it is not true that we are responsible for these problems.

5 For many years the local, state, and federal governments have encouraged industry to build new factories in the area. These factories are polluting our water and our air with chemical waste. The waste poisons the water and kills the fish.

6 Also, many new people have come to live here and work in the factories. In the summer, people from the city come to live here in vacation houses near the river. Now tons of raw sewage from their toilets are polluting the river.

7 The same government which allows these things to happen is telling us that we are the cause of the problem. Can we believe that the government is the guardian of the river? Should we listen when this government tells us to stop fishing in the Biramichi River?

Continued

8 If we stop fishing, our way of life will die. During the winter months we have no work. The factories are for city people, and are not part of our way of life. If we do not fish, what will we live on? Must we ask the government for welfare? Must we leave our land and move to the city?

9 Last year we took only half the number of fish that we usually take. We did this without any laws or government. We did this because we care about the land and the water, and we don't need laws to tell us how to do it.

10 We recommend that the Bureau of Commercial Fisheries take the following steps:

- Spend $2,000,000 on building a salmon hatchery, where our people can work to care for the young salmon and help them to grow;
- Ban the building of new factories and the expansion of old ones;
- Make the local town government spend some tax dollars on a sewage treatment plant that will treat the sewage before it goes into the river.

Jigsaw Activity 4: Saving the Biramichi River

Reading Skills Exercises

B

True, False, or ?

Write **T** if the statement is true, **F** if it is false, or **?** if you can't find the answer in your reading.

1. ______ There is a problem in the river.
2. ______ There are not enough fish in the river.
3. ______ The people who wrote this report are angry.
4. ______ They don't care about the fish in the river.
5. ______ They don't know what is causing the problems in the river.
6. ______ They have some solutions to the problems.
7. ______ They want the government to close the factories.
8. ______ They are Native Americans.

Find the Words

Find words in the reading to match the meanings below. Write the matching word or words on the line next to each meaning.

Paragraph 1:

1. a group of people who work together ______________________
2. a kind of fish ______________________

Paragraph 2:

3. speak for ______________________
4. the people who lived before us ______________________
5. people who looked after it ______________________
6. animals ______________________
7. want to take ______________________
8. from long ago ______________________

Paragraph 4:

9. we are the cause of ______________________

Paragraph 5:

10. making it dirty ______________________
11. makes it dangerous for the fish ______________________

Continued

Reading Skills Exercises *Continued*

B

Paragraph 6:

12. dirty water from the toilets ____________________

Paragraph 10:

13. actions ____________________
14. a place where they can care for the young fish ____________________
15. stop ____________________
16. a place where they can clean the water from the toilets ____________________
17. put ____________________

Find the Meaning

Find the words on the left in the reading. Then match each word to its meaning by checking (✔) a, b, or c. *Do not use a dictionary!*

Paragraph 1:

1. for many generations
   a. a long time
   b. a lot of people
   c. many families

Paragraph 5:

2. encouraged
   a. helped
   b. told
   c. gave them courage

Paragraph 10:

3. expansion
   a. making them smaller
   b. making them bigger
   c. making them stronger

Reading Skills Exercises *Continued*

B

Find the Details

List the problems in the Biramichi River. Then list the solutions that the Cooperative's members recommend.

Problems	Solutions
______________________	______________________
______________________	______________________
______________________	______________________
______________________	______________________

Think About It

Read the following questions and discuss them with your group. Then write your answers on the lines below.

Who will be unhappy about the solutions that the members of the Cooperative suggest? Why do you think so?

1. I think the ______________________ will be unhappy because
____
____
____
____
____

2. I think the ______________________ will be unhappy because
____
____
____
____
____

3. I think the ______________________ will be unhappy because
____
____
____
____
____

Jigsaw Activity 4
Saving the Biramichi River

C

Directions: Look at the picture below. How do you think the things in the picture are related to each other? How are they related to the title of the reading?

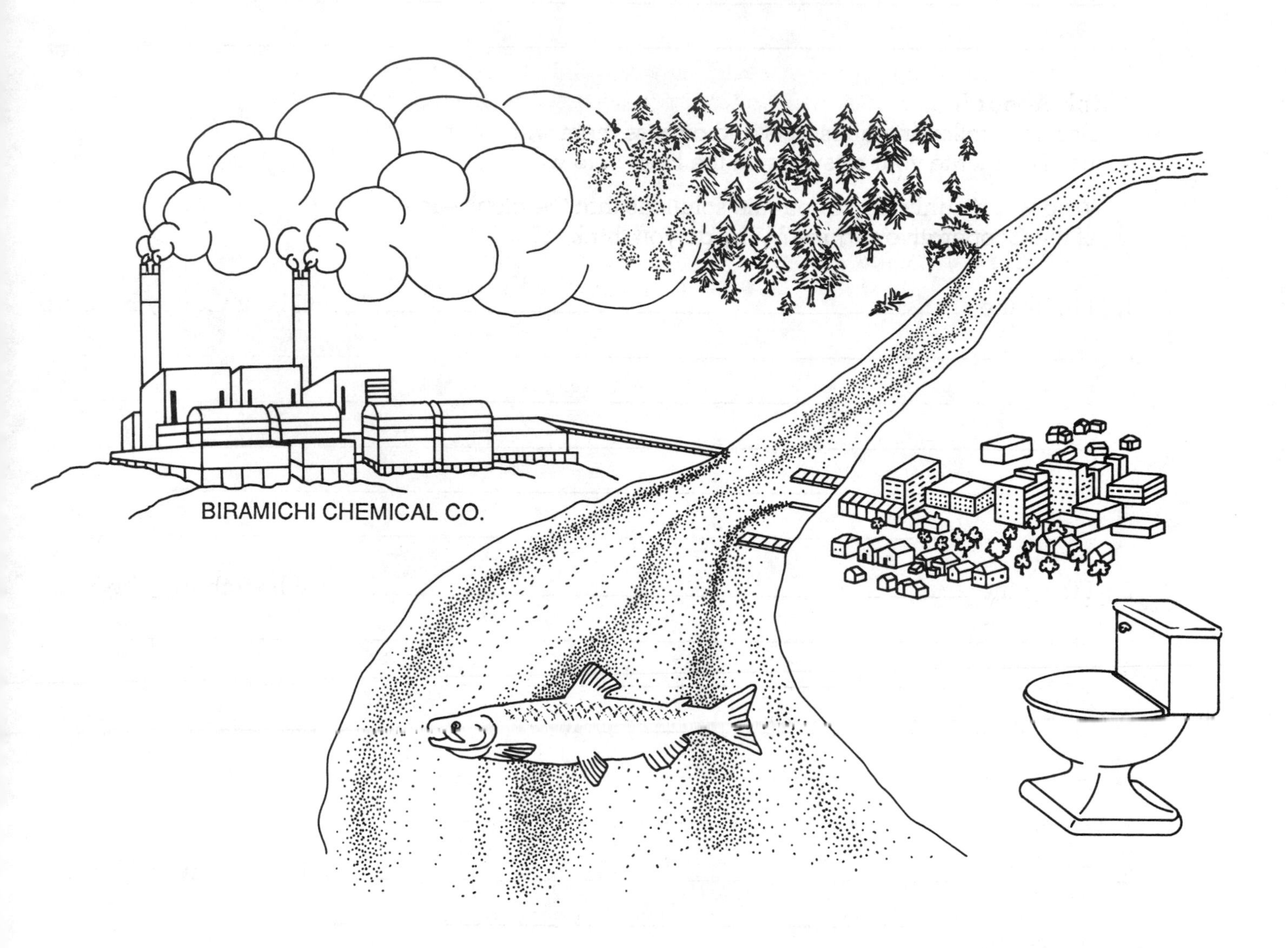

Reading

Directions: Read the story below and discuss it with your group.

1 There are some serious problems in the Biramichi River. Several groups have studied the problems. The local Chamber of Commerce, which represents the industries in the area, hired a consultant to study the problems and write a report for them. This is her report:

2 I was hired by the Biramichi Chamber of Commerce to do a one-year study on salmon fishing in the Biramichi River. This is a summary of my findings.

3 One of the major problems in the Biramichi River is that the level of oxygen in the water is too low. Several chemicals have displaced the oxygen. This chemical pollution has two sources: the factories, which dump polluted water directly into the river, and the local community, which dumps untreated human sewage into the river.

4 The local town government has already spent $2,000,000 on sewage treatment projects, but it would cost another $27,000,000 to complete the projects. It will take at least 15 years for the town to collect enough revenue from taxes to complete these projects.

5 The factories here employ 17,000 people, in an area where there is very little alternative employment. It is not economically practical to close or relocate the factories. Also, the factories cannot afford to finance chemical treatment plants by themselves.

6 Another problem is that the members of the Biramichi Fishing Cooperative are over-fishing. The salmon are caught when the fish are on their way upstream to spawn. Not enough fish are left to spawn and reproduce in large numbers.

7 The members of the Cooperative say that they have already reduced their annual catch by 50%. However, my studies indicate that they took fewer fish because there were fewer fish to catch, not because they were trying to preserve the salmon.

Continued

Reading *Continued*

8 My recommendations are:

- The Bureau of Commercial Fisheries should ban fishing until the number of salmon reaches a satisfactory level, probably four or five years from now.
- The Bureau of Commercial Fisheries should hire additional staff to patrol the river and control poachers who do not obey the ban.
- The local town government should apply to the federal Environmental Protection Agency for funds to help pay for the sewage treatment plants immediately.

Reading Skills Exercises

C

True, False, or ?

Write **T** if the statement is true, **F** if it is false, or **?** if you can't find the answer in your reading.

1. ______ The person who wrote this report is a factory owner.
2. ______ She was paid by the factory owners.
3. ______ This is her complete report.
4. ______ There is not enough oxygen in the water.
5. ______ She wants the factories to be closed.
6. ______ She trusts the fishers to obey the law about fishing.
7. ______ She says the factories should pay to clean up the river.
8. ______ Everyone in the area will be pleased with her recommendations.

Find the Words

Find words in the reading to match the meanings below. Write the matching word or words on the line next to each meaning.

Paragraph 2:

1. a kind of fish ______________________

Paragraph 3:

2. removed, destroyed ______________________
3. people who live there ______________________
4. waste from the toilets ______________________

Paragraph 4:

5. methods of cleaning it up ______________________
6. money ______________________

Paragraph 5:

7. other ______________________
8. move ______________________
9. a place where people can clean the chemicals out of the water ______________________

Continued

Reading Skills Exercises *Continued*

C

Paragraph 6:

10. a group that works together ____________________
11. taking too many fish ____________________
12. lay eggs ____________________

Paragraph 7:

13. the number they take each year ____________________
14. show us, tell us ____________________
15. save ____________________

Paragraph 8:

16. watch or guard ____________________
17. follow ____________________
18. money ____________________

Find the Meaning

Find the words on the left in the reading. Then match each word to its meaning by checking (✔) a, b, or c. *Do not use a dictionary!*

Paragraph 2:

1. findings
   a. something she found
   b. something she lost
   c. the results

Paragraph 3:

2. sources
   a. causes
   b. results
   c. places

Paragraph 5:

3. finance
   a. finish
   b. pay for
   c. plan

Paragraph 7:

4. reduced
   a. increased
   b. decreased
   c. changed

Continued

Reading Skills Exercises *Continued*

Paragraph 8:

5. ban
   a. stop
   b. reduce
   c. allow

6. poachers
   a. people who catch fish
   b. people who take too many fish
   c. people who steal fish

Find the Details

List the problems that the consultant found. Then list the solutions that she recommends.

Problems	Solutions
______________________	______________________
______________________	______________________
______________________	______________________
______________________	______________________

Think About It

Read the following questions and discuss them with your group. Then write your answers on the lines below.

A. Who will be unhappy about the solutions that the consultant suggests? Why do you think so?

1. I think the ______________________ will be unhappy because
____
____
____
____
____

2. I think the ______________________ will be unhappy because
____
____
____
____
____

Continued

Reading Skills Exercises *Continued*

3. I think the ____________________ will be unhappy because

____

B. Who will be happy with her recommendations? Why do you think so?

1. I think the ____________________ will be happy because

____

2. I think the ____________________ will be happy because

____

Jigsaw Activity 4
Saving the Biramichi River

D

Directions: Look at the picture below. How do you think the things in the picture are related to each other? How are they related to the title of the reading?

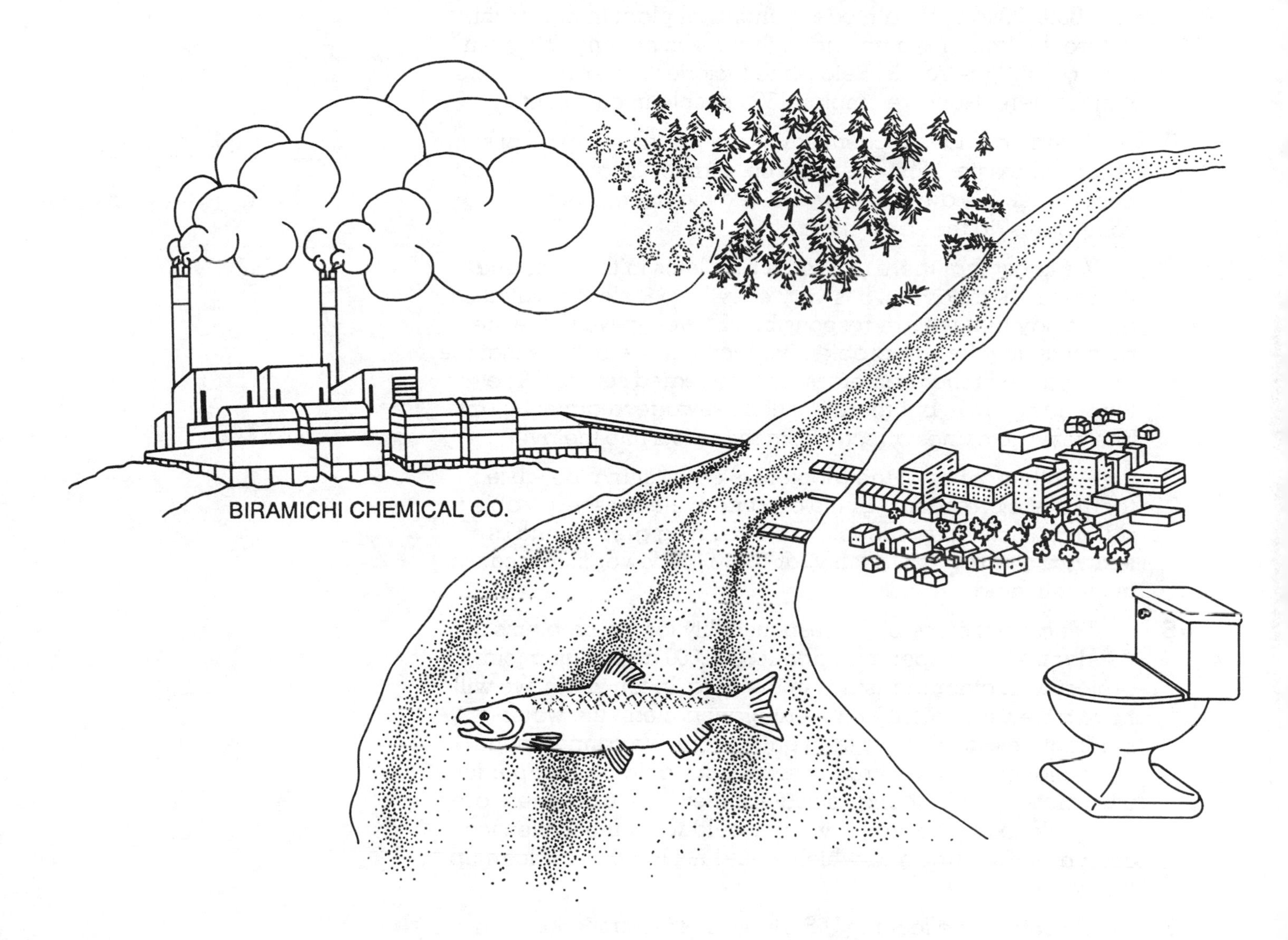

Jigsaw Activity 4: Saving the Biramichi River

Reading

Directions: Read the story below and discuss it with your group.

1 There are some serious problems in the Biramichi River. Several groups have studied the problems. This is the opinion of one of the companies in the area:

2 We are the Biramichi Chemical Company. We spent $100,000,000 to build a modern chemical plant in Biramichi. Before the factories came here, there was nothing. We even had to build the roads. Before the factories came, there were no jobs here. Now we employ 1500 people in our plant.

3 When you have a chemical plant, you must get rid of some chemical waste. Most chemical companies locate their plants near water. We dump our waste into the river. Other companies do the same thing.

4 We know that there are some problems in the river and that the fish are dying. It is very easy for people to point at us and to say that we are responsible. However, we share the responsibility for this problem with others. We believe that the main cause of the problem is raw, untreated sewage. The town has grown, but there is still no sewage treatment plant. The sewage comes directly from the toilets into the river.

5 Another cause of the problem is over-fishing. Because there are more people in the area now, the fishers are able to sell more fish. These people are becoming greedy, and are taking too many fish. Each year there are fewer fish because of over-fishing.

6 We accept some of the responsibility for the problems in the river. We are spending about $500,000 a year on a joint project with other industries in the area. In ten years, we will have a new chemical treatment plant to clean the water before it enters the river from our factory. We cannot spend more money to have it ready sooner. It would be cheaper for us to close the plant and relocate somewhere else. There are many places in the world which would welcome a chemical company like ours, and which would not force us to clean up the water.

7 Therefore, we feel the U.S. Bureau of Commercial Fisheries should take two steps:

- Ban fishing for five years so that the fish have a chance to reproduce and increase in number;
- Make the local town government spend money on a sewage treatment plant.

Reading Skills Exercises

D

True, False, or ?

Write **T** if the statement is true, **F** if it is false, or **?** if you can't find the answer in your reading.

1. _______ There is a problem in the river.
2. _______ The Biramichi Chemical Company says it is not responsible.
3. _______ It dumps chemicals into the river.
4. _______ It is the only factory that puts chemicals into the river.
5. _______ The water in the river is probably safe to drink.
6. _______ The Biramichi Chemical Company will close the factory.
7. _______ The company has some advice for the Bureau of Commercial Fisheries.
8. _______ Everyone in the area will be happy with the advice.

Find the Words

Find words in the reading to match the meanings below. Write the matching word or words on the line next to each meaning.

Paragraph 2:

1. factory _______________
2. give work to _______________

Paragraph 4:

3. we are causing the problem _______________
4. biggest _______________
5. human waste from the toilets _______________

Paragraph 5:

6. taking too many fish _______________

Paragraph 6:

7. building it together _______________
8. factories _______________
9. a place where people can clean the chemicals out of the water _______________
10. move to another place _______________

Continued

Reading Skills Exercises *Continued*

Paragraph 7:

11. actions ______________________
12. stop ______________________
13. lay their eggs ______________________
14. a place where they can clean the water from the toilets ______________________

Find the Meaning

Find the words on the left in the reading. Then match each word to its meaning by checking (✔) a, b, or c. *Do not use a dictionary!*

Paragraph 3:

1. locate
   - a. fix
   - b. build
   - c. find

Paragraph 4:

2. point at us
   - a. look at us
   - b. blame us
   - c. find us

3. we share the responsibility
   - a. we are not to blame
   - b. other people are to blame
   - c. we are partly to blame

Paragraph 5:

4. greedy
   - a. they want more to eat
   - b. they eat too much fish
   - c. they want too much money

Paragraph 6:

5. accept
   - a. agree to share
   - b. reject
   - c. take

Reading Skills Exercises *Continued*

D

Find the Details

List the problems that the chemical company found. Then list the solutions that the company suggests.

Problems	Solutions

Think About It

Read the following questions and discuss them with your group. Then write your answers on the lines below.

A. Who will be unhappy about the solutions that the company suggests? Why do you think so?

1. I think the ____________________ will be unhappy because

2. I think the ____________________ will be unhappy because

3. I think the ____________________ will be unhappy because

Continued

Reading Skills Exercises *Continued*

D

B. Some people will be worried about something that the company says in this report. Who? Why do you think so?

1. I think the ______________________ will be worried because
____
____
____
____
____

2. I think the ______________________ will be worried because
____
____
____
____
____

Name ______________________________

Jigsaw Activity 4

Saving the Biramichi River Quiz

Directions: Work alone to answer the questions below.

True or False?

Write **T** if the statement is true, **F** if the statement is false.

1. ______ The river is polluted.
2. ______ There are three causes of pollution.
3. ______ The factories brought jobs to the area.
4. ______ Most of the workers in the factories are Native Americans.
5. ______ Everyone agrees on what should be done to save the river.
6. ______ Everyone agrees that the town needs a sewage treatment plant.
7. ______ The town government has not given its opinion.
8. ______ The factories plan to build a chemical treatment plant immediately.
9. ______ The members of the Fishing Cooperative have agreed to stop fishing for three years.

What Do You Think?

You have read or heard the opinions of the National Bureau of Commercial Fisheries, the Biramichi Fishing Cooperative, the Biramichi Chemical Company, and the Biramichi Chamber of Commerce. Now give your opinion. Who is to blame for the problem? What should be done about it?

____

____

____

____

____

____

____

____

____

____

____

Personal Evaluation Sheet: Working in Groups

Now that you have been working in groups for a while, spend some time thinking about how well you work in a group. This self-evaluation form will help you to think about your group skills.

Directions: Read each statement below. Then circle the number that best represents what you did in your group.

	Yes, often.					No, not at all.
1. I talked to everyone in my group today.	5	4	3	2	1	0
2. I listened to everybody in my group today.	5	4	3	2	1	0
3. I encouraged and praised others in my group.	5	4	3	2	1	0
4. I explained to someone who didn't understand.	5	4	3	2	1	0
5. I asked for an explanation when I didn't understand.	5	4	3	2	1	0

Jigsaw Activity 5
Who Discovered America?

Directions: Look at the map below and discuss it with your group.

KEY

1. Norway
2. Iceland
3. Greenland
4. Newfoundland

Eric's father's journey - - - - - -
Eric's journey ————
Leif's journey — - — -

Jigsaw Activity 5: Who Discovered America?

Reading

Directions: Read the story below and discuss it with your group.

1 According to some ancient stories from northern Europe, Vikings came to North America almost 1000 years ago.

2 The Vikings were the people who lived in what we now call Scandinavia. They used to tell exciting stories about their history and their ancestors, who travelled the oceans and had many adventures. These stories were not written down at first; they were passed on orally from parent to child. The stories were called sagas, and the two most famous sagas were *The Greenlanders' Saga* and *Eric the Red's Saga*. Eventually, the sagas were written down, and scholars have studied and translated them.

3 Both of these sagas tell of a long voyage west from Iceland, where Eric the Red's family lived. According to some legends, the family came from Norway, but had to leave in a hurry when Eric's father got into serious trouble. They settled in Iceland. Later, Eric had to flee Iceland after he killed a man. He went to live in some islands in western Iceland. Even there he came into conflict with his neighbors. The local government was so angry with him that they banished him and his family. He could never return to Iceland. He had no other place to go, so he set out for the open sea to the west, hoping to find a land where he could settle.

4 He sailed across almost 200 miles of open sea, until he came to a huge, ice-covered land where there were no neighbors to quarrel with. He called it Greenland and sent back good reports so that other settlers would want to come there. Soon some other people did follow him and settled in Greenland.

5 One of the new settlers lost his way in bad weather. While he was heading west, he saw some unknown land in the distance. It appeared to have plenty of trees. When he finally arrived in Greenland, he told people about what he had seen.

6 One of those who heard the story was Leif Ericsson (Eric's son). He was very interested, because Greenland had very little wood. Life in Greenland would be much easier if they could get wood for building homes and furniture, and for burning as fuel to keep them warm. He could get very rich in this trade.

Continued

Reading *Continued*

7 Leif Ericsson and a crew of 35 sailors set off westward over the sea. The saga tells how he found this land. It was covered with forest. The rivers were full of fish, and the ground was covered with high grass which they could use to feed their livestock. They stayed there over the winter, and found it milder than the Greenland winter. They found a kind of berry which made good wine, and they called the land "Vinland," which meant "Wineland."

8 Because the sagas told of a mild climate, many scholars thought that Vinland must have been in what is now called New England, in the United States. But in the 1960s archeologists in Newfoundland, Canada, dug up the remains of a Viking settlement. The place matched the description in the sagas in every way but one: the climate.

9 Geographers and climatologists explain that the climate was different a thousand years ago, and some parts of the land are higher than they were then. This may explain why the sagas speak of a mild climate in Vinland, whereas Newfoundland now has severe winters.

10 Many archeologists and scholars are convinced that the settlement in Newfoundland was Leif Ericsson's Vinland. It is certain that Leif, or some other Viking explorer, arrived in Newfoundland more than 1000 years ago.

Reading Skills Exercises

True, False, or ?

Write **T** if the statement is true, **F** if it is false, or **?** if you can't find the answer in your reading.

1. ______ The Vikings discovered the continent of America.
2. ______ They sailed from Iceland to Canada.
3. ______ They came to find gold.
4. ______ Archeologists study the past.
5. ______ The Vikings liked the new land.
6. ______ Leif Ericsson wrote the story of his adventures.
7. ______ Newfoundland used to be warmer than it is now.

Find the Words

Find words in the reading to match the meanings below. Write the matching word or words on the line next to each meaning.

Paragraph 1:

1. very old; from long ago ______________________

Paragraph 2:

2. the people who lived in Scandinavia ______________________
3. people who lived long ago ______________________
4. told ______________________
5. later ______________________
6. people who study ______________________

Paragraph 3:

7. journey ______________________
8. stories about the past ______________________
9. run away ______________________
10. fighting and argument ______________________
11. sent him away ______________________
12. headed for ______________________
13. make a new home ______________________

Continued

Reading Skills Exercises *Continued*

Paragraph 7:

14. group of sailors ________________
15. farm animals ________________
16. warmer ________________

Paragraph 8:

17. people who study the past ________________
18. was the same ________________
19. weather ________________

Paragraph 9:

20. people who study the weather ________________
21. very cold ________________

Paragraph 10:

22. certain, sure ________________

Study the Map

Complete these sentences about the map on p. 127. Use words such as *north*, *south*, *east*, and *west* for some of your answers.

1. To reach Iceland, Eric's father had to sail ________________ from Norway.
2. Greenland is ________________ of Iceland.
3. Greenland is much bigger than ________________ .
4. Iceland is farther north than ________________ .
5. Newfoundland is a large island near the ________________ coast of North America.
6. When Leif left Greenland, he first sailed ________________ along the coast of ________________ . Then he turned ________________ and sailed along the coast of ________________ until he reached ________________ .

Continued

Reading Skills Exercises *Continued*

7. Eric's father's journey was the shortest; Eric's was
   ____________________, but Leif's journey was
   ____________________.

8. Greenland is much closer to the ____________________
   ____________________ than Newfoundland is. That is why
   Newfoundland's climate is ____________________ than the
   climate in Greenland.

Jigsaw Activity 5

Who Discovered America?

B

Directions: Look at the map below and discuss it with your group.

KEY

1. Britain (England, Scotland, and Wales)
2. Greenland
3. Labrador
4. Newfoundland
5. Maine

Route of John the Skillful

Jigsaw Activity 5: Who Discovered America?

Reading

B

Directions: Read the story below and discuss it with your group.

1 A Welsh sailor named John the Skillful discovered North America 17 years before Christopher Columbus, says a British expert.

2 For 50 years, Arthur Davies has wanted to know who reached America first. As a boy in Wales, he heard legends about a Welsh prince who travelled to America hundreds of years ago. He decided that all legends are partly true, so it was possible that there really was a Welsh sailor who went to America so long ago.

3 According to Davies, John the Skillful's real name was John Lloyd. Davies studied old documents in which Lloyd was called "the greatest mariner in all England." Davies says that Lloyd reached North America in 1475, and probably explored large parts of the continent. Davies found an old globe, made in 1536. On the globe, there was a point in northern Canada that said John the Skillful had reached there in about 1476.

4 According to Davies, Lloyd kept quiet about his adventures because there were many other people who were trying to sail around the world to Asia, and he didn't want to give away his secrets. Also, Lloyd's actions were illegal. He did not have the permission of the king of England to go and search for new lands. In addition, Lloyd was trading with Greenland. At that time, the king of England did not allow British traders to trade with Greenland. So Lloyd did not tell the world about his discovery.

5 Davies says that Lloyd finally told one person about his voyage to America. He told John Cabot. Cabot was an Italian mariner. The king of England hired him to find a northwestern route to China. Cabot never found a northwestern route to China, but he did arrive in North America in 1497, probably first in Maine or Nova Scotia. He also landed farther north, in a place that he named "New Found Land." First he thought he was in China, in east Asia, but later he realized that this was a new place. He never returned from his last voyage, but his sailors told the English king about his discoveries.

Jigsaw Activity 5: Who Discovered America?

Reading Skills Exercises

B

True, False, or ?

Write **T** if the statement is true, **F** if it is false, or **?** if you can't find the answer in your reading.

1. ______ Arthur Davies says John Lloyd reached America before Columbus.
2. ______ Arthur Davies is Welsh.
3. ______ The king of England sent John Lloyd to find new lands.
4. ______ John Lloyd never told anyone of his discovery.
5. ______ John Lloyd was a great sailor.
6. ______ John Lloyd's real name was John the Skillful.
7. ______ "Skillful" probably means that he was very good.
8. ______ Cabot found a northwestern route to China.
9. ______ Cabot told the English king about his discovery.

Find the Words

Find words in the reading to match the meanings below. Write the matching word or words on the line next to each meaning.

Paragraph 1:

1. from Wales ______________________________
2. found first ______________________________
3. someone who knows a lot ______________________________

Paragraph 2:

4. old stories ______________________________

Paragraph 3:

5. important papers ______________________________
6. sailor ______________________________
7. travelled through the new land ______________________________
8. a map like a ball ______________________________

Paragraph 4:

9. against the law ______________________________
10. buying and selling ______________________________

Paragraph 5:

11. a way to get there ______________________________

Reading Skills Exercises

B

Study the Map

Complete these sentences about the map on p. 133. Use words such as *north*, *south*, *east*, and *west* for some of your answers.

1. John the Skillful probably visited ____________________ before sailing to North America.
2. He sailed ____________________ from Britain to Greenland.
3. From Greenland, he sailed ____________________ to North America.
4. Then he sailed ____________________ along the coast of North America.
5. He sailed between Labrador and ____________________ .
6. Greenland is very cold, because it is near to the ____________________ ____________________.
7. When he left America, he sailed ____________________ to Britain.
8. He crossed the ____________________ ____________________ between Europe and America.
9. Greenland is ____________________ than North America, but ____________________ than Britain.

Jigsaw Activity 5
Who Discovered America?

Directions: Look at the map below and discuss it with your group.

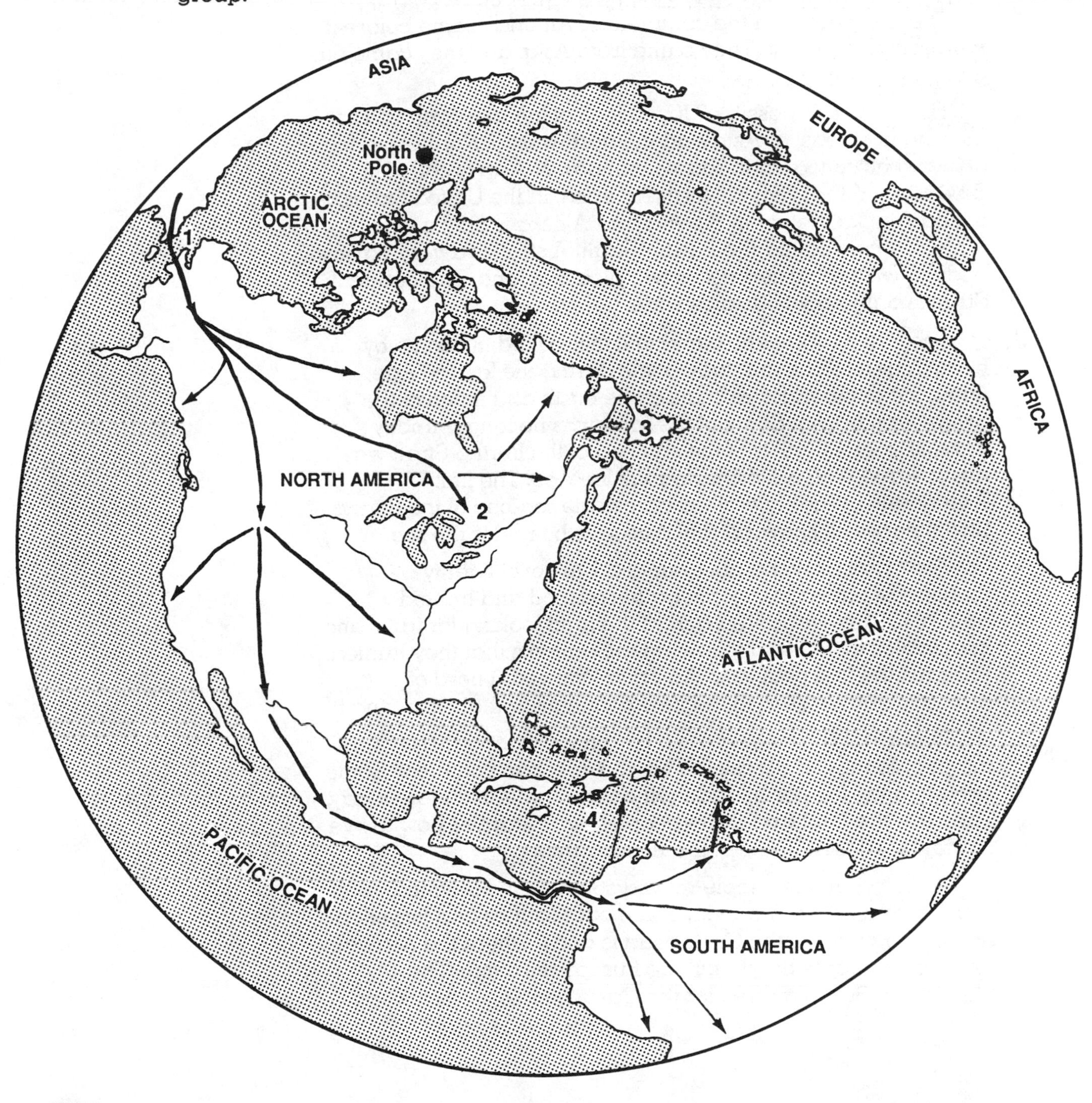

KEY

1. Bering Strait
2. Great Lakes
3. Newfoundland
4. Caribbean Sea

The travels of the native people

Jigsaw Activity 5: Who Discovered America?

Reading

Directions: Read the story below and discuss it with your group.

1 The first people in the continent of America came before it was called America. They came from Asia, and they came on foot.

2 How was this possible? If you look at the map, you will see that the northeast of Asia and the northwest of North America are very close together. Today, that part of Asia is called Siberia, and that part of North America, in the United States, is called Alaska. Between Siberia and Alaska is only a small body of water called the Bering Strait. A strait is a very narrow body of water that separates two pieces of land. The Bering Strait is only about 50 miles wide.

3 The first people who came to America did not come by boat. Experts think that they came during the last Ice Age, when ice covered large parts of the earth and much of the ocean was frozen. Some of the land was no longer under water. Experts think that the sea bed of the Bering Strait was not covered with water during the Ice Age. The first Americans probably walked across the sea bed of the Bering Strait, not even knowing that it used to be under the sea.

4 They probably did not plan to come here. Twenty thousand years ago, people gathered food and hunted animals. They wandered across the land looking for fruits and vegetables to eat, and following the animals that they hunted. Perhaps the first people in America followed a herd of animals, and crossed to the new continent without knowing it.

5 Twenty thousand years is a long time. During those years, the people moved across the North American continent. Some stayed in the far north, and their descendants live there today. They are the Inuit and Dene peoples, who learned how to live in the very cold climate of the Arctic Circle.

6 Other groups of people moved south. Some reached Central and South America. Some built canoes and travelled across the water to the Caribbean islands, where the Arawak and Carib people lived until the Europeans came. The Caribbean Sea is named for the Carib people.

Continued

Reading *Continued*

7 Other groups stayed in Central America. The Aztecs and the Mayans built great civilizations in Mexico. In North America, the people who stayed on the flat prairie land learned how to hunt buffalo and other animals. They lived according to their own laws until the Europeans came to the land. The people on the west and east coasts became great fishers and traders. The people of the woodlands became farmers who lived in permanent villages and had a very organized government.

8 When the Europeans arrived, they found that America was not an empty land. The people they found were not lost. The Europeans were not the first people to come to America; the native people discovered America 20,000 years ago.

Reading Skills Exercises

True, False, or ?

Write **T** if the statement is true, **F** if it is false, or **?** if you can't find the answer in your reading.

1. ______ The first people came to America by boat.
2. ______ They came from Asia.
3. ______ They came to find a new land for farming.
4. ______ They moved across the whole of North and South America.
5. ______ Their way of life changed after the Europeans came here.
6. ______ Their descendants are still here.

Find the Words

Find words in the reading to match the meanings below. Write the matching word or words on the line next to each meaning.

Paragraph 1:

1. they walked ______________________________

Paragraph 2:

2. a part of the sea ______________________________

Paragraph 3:

3. people who have studied this ______________________________
4. a time when almost the whole world was cold ______________________________
5. the bottom of the sea ______________________________

Paragraph 5:

6. the people who lived after them ______________________________
7. weather ______________________________
8. near the North Pole ______________________________

Paragraph 6:

9. small boats ______________________________

Continued

Paragraph 7:

10. flat land in the middle of North America ______________________
11. an animal that lived there ______________________
12. they stayed in one place ______________________

Paragraph 8:

13. the first people of America ______________________

Study the Map

Complete these sentences about the map on p. 137. Use words such as *north*, *south*, *east*, and *west* for some of your answers.

1. The native people crossed the ______________ from Asia to ______________.
2. Over many generations, they travelled in many different directions. Some travelled ______________ toward the Great Lakes.
3. Others went ______________ to settle beside the Pacific Ocean.
4. Other groups continued travelling ______________ toward South America.
5. Some groups travelled ______________ across the sea from South America to reach the islands in the ______________.
6. As they travelled south, the climate became ______________.
7. Those who stayed in the ______________ learned to live in Arctic conditions.

Jigsaw Activity 5
Who Discovered America?

Directions: Look at the map below and discuss it with your group.

KEY

1. Spain
2. Portugal
3. Canary Islands
4. Caribbean Sea

Columbus' voyage

Jigsaw Activity 5: Who Discovered America?

Reading

Directions: Read the story below and discuss it with your group.

1 Christopher Columbus was an Italian from the great port of Genoa. As a boy, he often talked with sailors in the port after their long and dangerous voyages across the ocean.

2 He became a sailor, and after one of his voyages he arrived in Portugal.

3 Lisbon, the capital city of Portugal, was one of the great centers of learning, exploration, and discovery in Europe. Columbus studied old maps and read the books of great geographers and travellers. He began to think that the world was round like a ball, not flat like a plate as most people then thought. He decided that it must be possible to sail around the world and not fall off.

4 At that time, Europeans were trading with China, India, and Japan. They had to travel overland, going east, to get there. The journey was long and dangerous, but traders made the journey because they could get very rich. Europeans would pay a lot of money for the spices, silks, and jewels of the East, or "the Indies" as they called it.

5 Columbus decided that he would try to get to the east by sailing in the opposite direction. If the world was round, he said, then if he kept sailing west he must eventually arrive in "the Indies." He estimated that the distance across the Atlantic would be about 2400 miles and that the voyage would take about three weeks.

6 Columbus was not a wealthy man. He had to find someone to sponsor him for the voyage. He needed money for ships, and he had to pay the crew. For two years Columbus begged the king of Portugal to sponsor him. However, the Portuguese finally decided to get to Asia by a different route, by sailing southeast around Africa. Then Columbus decided to try the king and queen of Spain. After six years, Queen Isabella agreed to be his sponsor.

7 After three months of preparation, in August 1492, Columbus set off with three ships—the Nina, the Pinta, and the Santa Maria—and a crew of about 90 sailors. They headed first for the Canary Islands. This first leg of the voyage took a week, but they had to stay there for three weeks while they made some repairs and got some final supplies. At last, on September 6, they set off into the unknown ocean to the west.

Continued

Reading *Continued*

8 Life on board the ship was rough. Only Columbus and the captains of the other two ships had beds; the sailors slept anywhere, in their clothes. They did the cooking on deck. They ate salt meat and fish, and mixed flour with seawater to make a kind of flat bread.

9 Columbus expected the journey to take about three weeks. Unfortunately, his calculations of the circumference of the world were not accurate. Some of the sailors wanted to turn back and go home. On October 12, they finally saw land.

10 Columbus and the other European navigators and geographers of the time did not know that America existed. When Columbus and his crew arrived at a Caribbean island, which they named San Salvador, they thought they were in "the Indies." Because they had reached "the Indies" by sailing west, they called the Caribbean lands "the West Indies," and they have had this name ever since. Columbus then called the people who lived there "Indians." The native people of the Americas are still called "Indians" today, but anthropologists call them "Amerindians" to show the difference from the Indians of India.

11 Until the day he died, Columbus thought he had arrived in "the Indies." He did not know that this was a whole continent that the Europeans would eventually call "America."

12 We know a lot about Columbus' voyage because he kept a journal in which he wrote a record of everything he did and saw. He had to keep accounts for the Spanish king and queen. Spain became very rich and powerful from the land and gold they found in America. They kept records and wrote history books that gave the Spanish point of view. For these reasons, many people think that Columbus discovered America.

Reading Skills Exercises

D

True, False, or ?

Write **T** if the statement is true, **F** if it is false, or **?** if you can't find the answer in your reading.

1. _______ Christopher Columbus was Spanish.
2. _______ The Europeans didn't know about America.
3. _______ Columbus wanted to sail to "the Indies."
4. _______ It took eight years to find a sponsor.
5. _______ The Portuguese sponsored Columbus' voyage.
6. _______ Columbus named the new land "America."
7. _______ Columbus made a mistake.
8. _______ Columbus discovered America.

Find the Words

Find words in the reading to match the meanings below. Write the matching word or words on the line next to each meaning.

Paragraph 1:

1. a city where ships come in _______________
2. a journey by sea _______________

Paragraph 3:

3. travelling to find new lands _______________
4. people who study the shape and size of the world _______________

Paragraph 4:

5. buying and selling _______________

Paragraph 5:

6. calculated _______________

Paragraph 6:

7. give him the money _______________
8. a group of sailors _______________

Continued

Reading Skills Exercises *Continued*

Paragraph 7:

9. started on a trip ______
10. part of a journey ______
11. fixed things ______
12. food, clothing, etc. ______

Paragraph 8:

13. difficult ______
14. leaders of ships ______

Paragraph 9:

15. the distance around it ______
16. mathematics ______
17. correct ______

Paragraph 10:

18. people who study the different people of the world ______

Paragraph 11:

19. later ______

Paragraph 12:

20. a kind of notebook ______
21. wrote down everything that happened ______
22. wrote down how much money he spent ______
23. way of looking at things ______

Continued

Reading Skills Exercises *Continued*

Study the Map

Complete these sentences about the map on p. 142. Use words such as *north*, *south*, *east*, and *west* for some of your answers.

1. Columbus first sailed ____________________ to the Canary Islands.
2. The Canary Islands are near the ____________________ coast of Africa.
3. He sailed across the ____________________ ____________________ to reach America.
4. He did not reach the mainland of the American continent. He reached some islands in the ____________________, which is ____________________ of America.
5. When he sailed home, he took a route farther ____________________ than he did on his outward journey.
6. When he returned to Europe, he arrived in ____________________, although he had left from ____________________.
7. Portugal is ____________________ than Spain.
8. Spain is ____________________ to Africa than Portugal is.

Name ________________________________

Jigsaw Activity 5
Who Discovered America? Quiz

Directions: Work alone to answer the questions below.

True or False?

Write **T** if the statement is true, **F** if the statement is false.

1. ______ The Vikings came to North America to search for gold.
2. ______ Leif Ericsson wrote the story of his adventures.
3. ______ The native people came from India.
4. ______ The native people are Amerindians.
5. ______ John the Skillful was hired by the king of England to find new lands.
6. ______ Columbus was working for the king and queen of Spain.
7. ______ The Europeans were looking for a way to get to the East.
8. ______ Columbus made some mistakes.
9. ______ The native people were the first people in America.
10. ______ We can study history only through written records and documents.

Complete the Sentences

Complete each of the sentences with a word from the list below. Use each word only once.

scholar	archeologist	mariner	expert
anthropologist	geographer	navigator	ancestors
settler	climatologist	explorer	descendants
trader	sponsor		

1. A ____________________ is a sailor.
2. An ____________________ is someone who knows a lot about something.
3. An ____________________ travels to new places.
4. Our ____________________ lived before us.
5. Our ____________________ will live after us.
6. A ____________________ is someone who buys and sells things.

Jigsaw Activity 5: Who Discovered America?

Quiz

7. An ____________________ looks for history in the ground.

8. A ____________________ knows a lot about the world.

9. A ____________________ goes to live in a new place.

10. A ____________________ agrees to pay for or support someone else.

11. A ____________________ studies the weather.

12. An ____________________ studies the different people of the world.

13. A ____________________ reads maps and guides ships on a voyage.

14. A ____________________ spends a lifetime studying.

What Do You Think?

1. Did Columbus discover America? Give reasons for your opinion.

____

____

____

____

____

____

2. Why are the native people called "Indians"?

____

____

____

____

Jigsaw Activity 5: Who Discovered America?

Quiz

Complete the Key

Identify the numbered places on the map below. Write your answers on the lines provided.

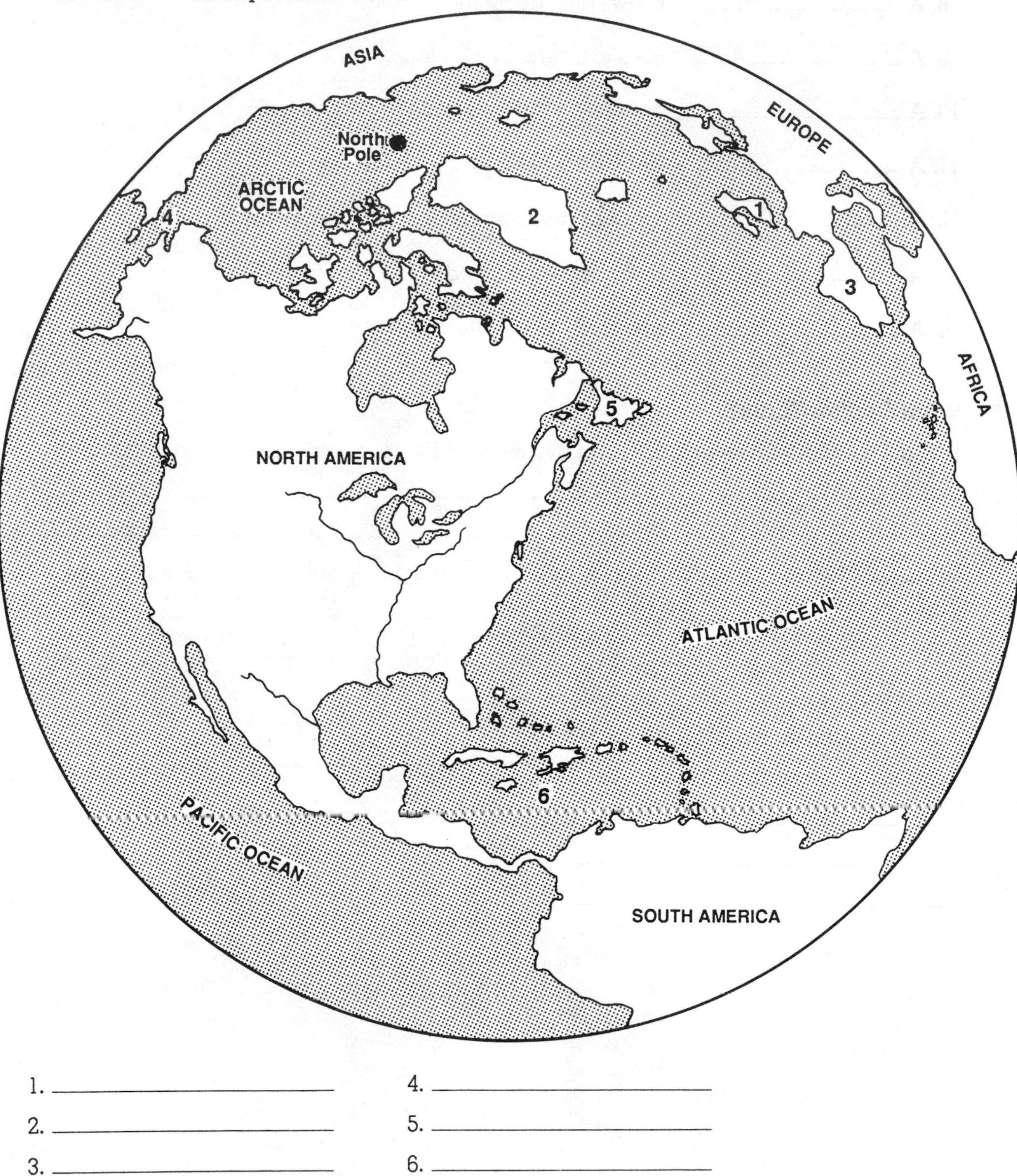

1. ______________________
2. ______________________
3. ______________________
4. ______________________
5. ______________________
6. ______________________

Answer Key

Jigsaw Activity 1

The Letter of the Law

Text A (pp. 50–51)

Complete the Sentences

1. how to use a transfer/how the SMTC works, etc. **2.** transportation/vehicles **3.** flat-fare **4.** transfer

Text B (pp. 52–53)

1. a problem on a bus/a boy who didn't get a transfer, etc. **2.** transfer **3.** followed the letter of the law

Text C (pp. 54–55)

1. a problem on the bus/a child who had to walk home, etc. **2.** transfer **3.** unkind and unreasonable **4.** complain

Text D (pp. 56–57)

1. the rules for using transfers/a problem on the bus, etc. **2.** full story **3.** obeyed **4.** everything is running properly/passengers and employees are following the rules, etc.

Quiz (p. 58)

True or False?

1. T **2.** F **3.** T **4.** F **5.** F **6.** F **7.** F **8.** F **9.** F **10.** T

What Do You Think?

Answers will vary. Accept all well-reasoned suggestions.

Jigsaw Activity 2

Heart Victim Can't Stay

Text A (pp. 60–63)

True, False, or ?

1. T **2.** ? **3.** T **4.** T **5.** F **6.** T **7.** T **8.** T

Find the Words

1. sweetheart **2.** immigrated **3.** (visitor's) visa **4.** expired **5.** eventually **6.** operation/attention **7.** replace **8.** facilities **9.** contacted **10.** officials **11.** I was desperate **12.** (immigration) officials **13.** apply for **14.** to my grave **15.** beg **16.** consider my case **17.** interpret the law with discretion

Think About It

Students' responses will vary.

Text B (pp. 64–67)

True, False, or ?

1. T **2.** T **3.** F **4.** F or ? **5.** T **6.** F **7.** T

Find the Words

1. (visitor's) visa **2.** set up house together **3.** operation **4.** expired **5.** is requesting **6.** extension **7.** permanent resident **8.** emergency **9.** genuine **10.** apply for **11.** spouse **12.** joint **13.** permits **14.** sponsor **15.** accept **16.** applicants **17.** security

Think About It

Students' responses will vary.

Text C (pp. 68–71)

True, False, or ?

1. F **2.** T **3.** T **4.** F **5.** ? **6.** F **7.** T

Find the Words

1. immigrated **2.** sweetheart **3.** expired **4.** settle **5.** supporting **6.** final **7.** replace **8.** operation **9.** proper facilities **10.** immigration officials **11.** extension **12.** declaration **13.** stick to the letter of the law **14.** inhuman **15.** consider his case **16.** interpret the law with discretion

Think About It

Students' responses will vary.

Text D (pp. 72–75)

True, False, or ?

1. T **2.** T **3.** F **4.** T **5.** ? **6.** F **7.** ? **8.** T

Find the Words

1. (cardiovascular) surgeon **2.** patient **3.** advised him **4.** replace **5.** facilities **6.** confirmed (the diagnosis) **7.** mitral valve disease **8.** failure **9.** the patient has been informed **10.** be responsible for the cost **11.** extend his visa **12.** schedule **13.** survival **14.** slim **15.** he is likely to **16.** reconsider

Think About It

Students' responses will vary.

Quiz (p. 76)

True or False?

1. F **2.** T **3.** T **4.** F **5.** F **6.** T **7.** F **8.** T **9.** T **10.** T

What Do You Think?

Students' responses will vary, but students should refer to the facts in the story to support their opinions.

Jigsaw Activity 3

Industrial Accident

Text A (pp. 79–82)

continued on next page

Jigsaw Activity 3 continued

Industrial Accident

True, False, or ?

1. F **2.** T **3.** ?, or students may infer F from the evidence about the smell and the explosion **4.** ?, or students may infer T from the evidence about the smell and the explosion **5.** ?

Find the Words

1. plant **2.** furnace **3.** operator **4.** supervisor **5.** burner **6.** bell **7.** flash **8.** ambulance

Think About It

Answers will vary. Opinions should be supported with references to the text.

Text B (pp. 83–88)

True, False, or ?

1. T **2.** F **3.** T **4.** F **5.** F or ? **6.** T

Find the Words

1. injured **2.** investigator **3.** protest **4.** put us all out of business **5.** processing **6.** transfer **7.** skills **8.** does not have the capacity **9.** shifts **10.** working under pressure **11.** risk **12.** steps be taken **13.** invest in **14.** equipment **15.** expansion **16.** accident prevention **17.** at the company's expense **18.** negotiate **19.** benefits

Think About It

Answers will vary. Opinions should be supported with references to the text.

Text C (pp. 89–92)

True, False, or ?

1. F **2.** T or ? **3.** T **4.** Opinions will vary **5.** ? **6.** T

Find the Words

1. investigated **2.** plant **3.** furnace **4.** blown up **5.** injured **6.** scene **7.** the temperature increased **8.** not to blame

Think About It

Answers will vary. Opinions should be supported with references to the text.

Text D (pp. 93–97)

True, False, or ?

1. T **2.** T **3.** F **4.** ? **5.** T **6.** F **7.** F

Find the Words

1. supervisor **2.** foundry **3.** willing **4.** goes too far **5.** crane **6.** prevent **7.** occasionally **8.** memo **9.** maintenance department **10.** ambulance **11.** plastic surgery

Think About It

Answers will vary. Opinions should be supported with references to the text.

Quiz (p. 98)

True or False?

1. F **2.** F **3.** F **4.** T **5.** F **6.** F **7.** F **8.** T **9.** F **10.** T

What Do You Think?

Answers will vary. Accept all well-reasoned answers based on information from all four readings and on inferences that can be made beyond the text.

Jigsaw Activity 4

Saving the Biramichi River

Text A (pp. 101–105)

True, False, or ?

1. T **2.** T **3.** F **4.** F **5.** T **6.** F **7.** T **8.** ?

Find the Words

1. salmon **2.** improve **3.** identify **4.** human sewage **5.** residents **6.** estimate **7.** polluted water/pollution **8.** over-fishing **9.** set quotas **10.** is responsible for **11.** solutions **12.** sewage treatment plants **13.** factories **14.** ban

Find the Meaning

1. a. **2.** c. **3.** c. **4.** a. **5.** b.

Find the Details

Problems: sewage; chemical pollution; over-fishing. Solutions: sewage treatment plants; stop the factories from pouring polluted water into the river; ban fishing for three years.

Think About It

Residents: they will have to pay for the plant out of their taxes. Factory owners: they will have to find some other way to get rid of the pollution. Fishers: they will not be able to make a living.

Text B (pp. 106–111)

True, False, or ?

1. T **2.** T **3.** T **4.** F **5.** F **6.** T **7.** F **8.** T

Find the Words

1. Cooperative **2.** salmon **3.** represent **4.** ancestors **5.** guardians **6.** wildlife **7.** claim **8.** traditional **9.** we are responsible **10.** polluting **11.** poisons **12.** sewage **13.** steps **14.** hatchery **15.** ban **16.** sewage treatment plant **17.** dump

Find the Meaning

1. a. **2.** a. **3.** b.

Find the Details

Problems: fewer salmon; chemical pollution; sewage. Solutions: salmon hatchery; ban the building or expansion of factories; build sewage treatment plant.

Think About It

Bureau of Commercial Fisheries: they will have to spend money on a salmon hatchery. Factory owners: they can't build or expand factories. Local government: it will have to spend money on a sewage treatment plant.

Text C (pp. 112–118)

True, False, or ?

1. F **2.** T **3.** F **4.** T **5.** F **6.** F **7.** F **8.** ?

Find the Words

1. salmon **2.** displaced **3.** residents **4.** sewage **5.** sewage treatment projects **6.** revenue **7.** alternative **8.** relocate **9.** chemical treatment plants **10.** cooperative **11.** over-fishing **12.** spawn **13.** annual catch **14.** indicate **15.** preserve **16.** patrol **17.** obey **18.** funds

Find the Meaning

1. c. **2.** a. **3.** b. **4.** b. **5.** a. **6.** c.

Find the Details

Problems: chemical pollution; sewage; over-fishing. Solutions: no solution to chemical pollution; apply for EPA funds to pay for sewage treatment plant; ban fishing for five years.

Think About It

A. Cooperative: they will not be able to catch fish. EPA: they will have to pay for the sewage treatment plant. Bureau of Commercial Fisheries: they will have to pay to enforce the ban. **B.** Local government: it will get funds from the EPA. Factories: they will remain open and receive financial assistance for their chemical treatment plants.

Text D (pp. 119–124)

True, False, or ?

1. T **2.** F **3.** T **4.** F **5.** ? or F **6.** ? or F **7.** T **8.** ?

Find the Words

1. plant **2.** employ **3.** we are responsible **4.** main **5.** sewage **6.** over-fishing **7.** a joint project **8.** industries **9.** chemical treatment plant **10.** relocate **11.** steps **12.** ban **13.** reproduce **14.** sewage treatment plant

Find the Meaning

1. c. **2.** b. **3.** c. **4.** c. **5.** c.

Find the Details

Problems: sewage; over-fishing; chemicals in the water. Solutions: local government should spend money on a sewage treatment plant; ban fishing for five years; chemical treatment plant ready in ten years.

Think About It

A. Fishers: they will not be able to fish. Local government: it will have to spend money on a sewage treatment plant. **B.** Workers: they may lose their jobs if Biramichi Chemical Company relocates.

Quiz (p. 125)

True or False?

1. T **2.** F **3.** T **4.** F **5.** F **6.** T **7.** T **8.** F **9.** F

What Do You Think?

Answers will vary. Accept all reasonable suggestions.

Jigsaw Activity 5

Who Discovered America?

Text A (pp. 127–132)

True, False, or ?

1. ? **2.** F **3.** F **4.** T **5.** T **6.** F **7.** T

Find the Words

1. ancient **2.** Vikings **3.** ancestors **4.** passed orally **5.** eventually **6.** scholars **7.** voyage **8.** legends **9.** flee **10.** conflict **11.** banished **12.** set out for **13.** settle **14.** crew **15.** livestock **16.** milder **17.** archeologists **18.** matched **19.** climate **20.** climatologists **21.** severe **22.** convinced

Study the Map

1. west **2.** west **3.** Iceland **4.** Newfoundland **5.** east **6.** north, Greenland, south, North America, Newfoundland **7.** longer, the longest **8.** North Pole, milder/warmer

Text B (pp. 133–136)

True, False, or ?

1. T **2.** T or ? **3.** F **4.** F **5.** T **6.** F **7.** T **8.** F **9.** F

continued on next page

Jigsaw Activity 5 continued

Who Discovered America?

Find the Words

1. Welsh **2.** discovered **3.** expert **4.** legends **5.** documents **6.** mariner **7.** explored **8.** globe **9.** illegal **10.** trading **11.** route

Study the Map

1. Greenland **2.** northwest **3.** west **4.** south **5.** Newfoundland **6.** North Pole **7.** east **8.** Atlantic Ocean **9.** smaller, larger

Text C (pp. 137–141)

True, False, or ?

1. F **2.** T **3.** F **4.** T **5.** T or ? **6.** T or ?

Find the Words

1. came on foot **2.** strait **3.** experts **4.** Ice Age **5.** sea bed **6.** descendants **7.** climate **8.** Arctic Circle **9.** canoes **10.** prairie **11.** buffalo **12.** in permanent villages **13.** native people

Study the Map

1. Bering Strait, America/North America **2.** southeast **3.** southwest **4.** south **5.** northeast, Caribbean Sea **6.** warmer **7.** north/Arctic Circle

Text D (pp. 142–147)

True, False, or ?

1. F **2.** T **3.** T **4.** T **5.** F **6.** F **7.** T **8.** F or ?

Find the Words

1. port **2.** voyage **3.** exploration **4.** geographers **5.** trading **6.** estimated **7.** sponsor **8.** crew **9.** set off **10.** leg **11.** made repairs **12.** supplies **13.** rough **14.** captains **15.** circumference **16.** calculations **17.** accurate **18.** anthropologists **19.** eventually **20.** journal **21.** wrote a record **22.** kept accounts **23.** point of view

Study the Map

1. south **2.** west **3.** Atlantic Ocean **4.** Caribbean Sea, east **5.** north **6.** Portugal, Spain 7. smaller **8.** closer/nearer

Quiz (pp. 149–150)

True or False ?

1. F **2.** F **3.** F **4.** T **5.** F **6.** T **7.** T **8.** T **9.** T **10.** F

Complete the Sentences

1. mariner **2.** expert **3.** explorer **4.** ancestors **5.** descendants **6.** trader **7.** archeologist **8.** geographer **9.** settler **10.** sponsor **11.** climatologist **12.** anthropologist **13.** navigator **14.** scholar

What Do You Think?

Answers will vary, but they should refer to facts from the texts.

Complete the Key

1. Great Britain **2.** Greenland **3.** Spain **4.** Bering Strait **5.** Newfoundland **6.** Caribbean Sea